CU00943906

We hope this book has been informative and helpful on your journey to understanding and celebrating older adults. Thank you for your interest and support!

Title: Democracy in Action: Western Democracies and Challenges
Subtitle: Exploring the Intricacies of Democratic Governance and Contemporary Challenges

Series: Global Perspectives: Exploring World Politics
By Jonathan A. Sinclair

Table of Contents

Introduction **6**

Significance of Western Democracies in Global Politics... 6

Historical Evolution of Democratic Systems 10

Challenges Faced by Democratic Nations 14

Chapter 1: United States **18**

Overview of the U.S. Political System 18

Presidential vs. Parliamentary Systems 22

Electoral Process and Voting Systems 26

Political Parties and Partisan Politics 30

Chapter 2: United Kingdom **34**

Westminster System and Parliamentary Democracy 34

Role of the Monarchy and Constitutional Monarchy 39

Devolution and Regional Politics 43

Brexit and its Implications 47

Chapter 3: Germany **51**

Federal Republic and Consensus Politics 51

Coalition Governments and Multi-party System 55

Electoral Reforms and Proportional Representation 59

Impact of Historical Legacies on German Politics 63

Chapter 4: France **67**

Semi-Presidential System and Presidential Powers 67

Political Ideologies and Party System 72

Electoral Laws and French Electoral Process 76

Challenges of Immigration and Identity Politics *80*

Chapter 5: Challenges to Democracy **84**

Rise of Populism and its Impact on Western Democracies

....*84*

Political Polarization and Gridlock..................................*88*

Threats to Freedom of Press and Media..........................*92*

Electoral Reform Debates and Democratic Innovations 96

Chapter 6: Democratic Institutions and Civil Society

.... **100**

Role of Judiciary and Rule of Law..................................*100*

Checks and Balances in Western Democracies *104*

Role of Civil Society Organizations and Interest Groups

....*108*

Importance of a Free and Independent Judiciary *113*

Chapter 7: Democratic Governance in the Digital

Age **117**

Impact of Technology on Democracy and Elections......*117*

Social Media and Political Campaigns...........................*121*

Challenges of Cybersecurity and Election Interference 125

Balancing Privacy and Security in the Digital Era.......*130*

Conclusion **135**

Recap of Key Insights on Western Democracies...........*135*

Future of Democracy and Potential Reforms................*140*

Importance of Citizen Engagement and Democratic Participation *145*

Key Terms and Definitions **149**

Supporting Materials **153**

Introduction
Significance of Western Democracies in Global Politics

Western democracies have played a significant role in shaping the course of global politics for centuries. With their emphasis on individual freedoms, the rule of law, and representative governance, these nations have served as beacons of democratic values and have influenced political systems around the world. In this chapter, we will delve into the profound significance of Western democracies in global politics, examining their historical contributions, geopolitical influence, and soft power projection.

1. Historical Contributions to Democracy

To understand the significance of Western democracies in global politics, it is crucial to recognize their historical contributions to the development of democratic ideals. From ancient Greece, where the concept of democracy first emerged, to the Enlightenment era, which championed the principles of liberty and equality, Western civilizations have been at the forefront of shaping democratic thought. The Magna Carta, the American Revolution, and the French Revolution are all milestones that laid the foundation for modern democratic systems and influenced democratic movements worldwide.

2. Geopolitical Influence and Global Leadership

Western democracies have consistently played key roles as global leaders, exerting influence on international affairs through diplomatic relations, economic partnerships, and military alliances. Nations like the United States, the United Kingdom, Germany, and France have been at the forefront of promoting democratic values and human rights, advocating for peace and stability, and addressing global challenges such as climate change and poverty. Their political, economic, and military power has granted them a unique position on the global stage, enabling them to shape the international agenda and foster cooperation among nations.

3. Soft Power Projection and Cultural Influence

In addition to their geopolitical influence, Western democracies have exerted soft power through their cultural contributions and the export of democratic values. Western cultural products, including literature, music, films, and technological innovations, have reached global audiences and often become symbols of freedom, creativity, and progress. The ideals of individual liberty, equality, and human rights espoused by Western democracies have resonated with people worldwide, inspiring democratic movements and demanding political change in autocratic regimes.

4. Economic Powerhouses and Democratic Model

Many Western democracies have emerged as economic powerhouses, with robust market economies and high standards of living. These successful democratic models have demonstrated the compatibility of political freedom and economic prosperity, attracting admiration and emulation from nations seeking to strengthen their own democratic institutions. The Western democracies' ability to balance individual freedoms with social welfare, entrepreneurship with regulation, and economic growth with environmental sustainability has made them models for economic development around the world.

5. Democratic Alliances and Multilateral Cooperation

Western democracies have forged alliances and engaged in multilateral cooperation to address global challenges. Institutions such as NATO, the European Union, and the United Nations have been instrumental in fostering dialogue, promoting peace and security, and advancing democratic norms and values. These alliances have provided platforms for Western democracies to collaborate, share best practices, and jointly address issues such as terrorism, nuclear proliferation, and human rights violations.

Conclusion

The significance of Western democracies in global politics cannot be overstated. Their historical contributions, geopolitical influence, soft power projection, economic success, and commitment to democratic values have positioned them as influential players on the global stage. Western democracies have served as inspirations and models for nations seeking political change and have played key roles in shaping the international agenda. Understanding their significance is crucial for comprehending the challenges they face in the 21st century and the ongoing quest to strengthen and uphold democratic principles worldwide.

Historical Evolution of Democratic Systems

The evolution of democratic systems over centuries has shaped the political landscape of Western democracies and influenced political systems worldwide. In this chapter, we will embark on a journey through history to explore the origins, development, and transformation of democratic systems. By understanding the historical evolution of democracy, we can gain insights into the complexities and achievements of Western democracies today.

1. Ancient Roots of Democracy

The roots of democracy can be traced back to ancient civilizations, particularly ancient Greece. In Athens, the concept of direct democracy emerged, where citizens had a voice in decision-making through open assemblies. This early form of democracy laid the groundwork for democratic principles such as citizen participation and deliberation, although it was limited to a small segment of the population.

2. Enlightenment and the Birth of Modern Democracy

The Enlightenment period of the 17th and 18th centuries marked a significant turning point in the evolution of democratic thought. Philosophers such as John Locke, Montesquieu, and Jean-Jacques Rousseau introduced groundbreaking ideas on natural rights, social contract theory, and separation of powers. Their works influenced the

American and French Revolutions, which led to the establishment of constitutional democracies, with the United States adopting a representative democracy and France transitioning to a republic.

3. Expansion of Suffrage and Popular Movements

During the 19th and 20th centuries, Western democracies witnessed the expansion of suffrage rights and the rise of popular movements advocating for broader political participation. The fight for universal suffrage and the women's suffrage movement resulted in more inclusive and representative democratic systems. Additionally, labor movements, civil rights movements, and other social movements played pivotal roles in advancing democratic values and pushing for social justice.

4. Challenges and Transformations in the 20th Century

The 20th century presented significant challenges and transformations for Western democracies. The two World Wars tested democratic systems' resilience, with many nations facing the rise of authoritarian regimes. However, democratic ideals prevailed, leading to the defeat of totalitarianism. The post-war period witnessed the establishment of democratic institutions and the spread of democracy through decolonization movements.

5. Consolidation and Modern Challenges

In the latter half of the 20th century, Western democracies experienced a period of consolidation, where democratic institutions solidified and democratic norms became deeply ingrained. This period also saw the expansion of economic interdependence, the rise of globalization, and the impact of technological advancements, which presented new challenges and complexities for democratic systems.

6. Democratic Waves and Transitions

The end of the Cold War in the late 20th century marked a new era for democratic transitions, with the spread of democracy to formerly authoritarian regimes. Countries in Eastern Europe, Latin America, and parts of Africa and Asia embarked on democratic transitions, inspired by the success of Western democracies and the desire for political freedom and human rights.

7. Contemporary Democratic Dilemmas

In the 21st century, Western democracies face a range of challenges that test the strength and adaptability of their democratic systems. These challenges include rising populism, political polarization, the erosion of trust in institutions, the influence of money in politics, and the impact of digital technologies on political processes.

Addressing these dilemmas requires constant vigilance, innovation, and a commitment to democratic principles.

Conclusion

The historical evolution of democratic systems reveals the progress, achievements, and ongoing struggles of Western democracies. From ancient roots in Athens to the Enlightenment era, suffrage movements, and contemporary challenges, democratic systems have evolved and adapted to societal changes. Understanding this historical trajectory provides a foundation for comprehending the complexities and dynamics of Western democracies and highlights the need for continuous engagement and reform to uphold democratic values in the 21st century.

Challenges Faced by Democratic Nations

Democracies, while resilient and adaptive, face a multitude of challenges in the 21st century. In this chapter, we will explore the complex landscape of challenges faced by Western democracies, including internal and external factors that test the viability and effectiveness of democratic systems. Understanding these challenges is crucial for safeguarding and strengthening democratic principles in the face of evolving circumstances.

1. Rise of Populism and Democratic Backsliding

One of the significant challenges faced by democratic nations is the rise of populism, characterized by the emergence of charismatic leaders who often exploit social divisions and grievances. Populist movements can undermine democratic institutions, erode the checks and balances system, and propagate authoritarian tendencies. The erosion of democratic norms and the threat of democratic backsliding pose significant challenges to the stability and functionality of democratic systems.

2. Political Polarization and Gridlock

Political polarization, fueled by ideological differences and partisan divisions, presents a substantial challenge to democratic nations. When political parties and the electorate become increasingly polarized, it hampers the ability to find common ground and compromises necessary for effective governance. Gridlock in decision-making processes can lead to policy stagnation, exacerbate social tensions, and erode public trust in democratic institutions.

3. Threats to Freedom of Press and Media

The freedom of the press and an independent media are fundamental pillars of democratic societies. However, in recent years, democratic nations have faced challenges such as increasing censorship, attacks on journalists, and the spread of misinformation. These threats to press freedom undermine the public's access to accurate information, hinder democratic discourse, and weaken the ability of citizens to make informed decisions.

4. Electoral Reform Debates and Democratic Innovations

Democratic nations continually grapple with debates on electoral reforms to ensure fair and representative systems. Issues such as gerrymandering, campaign financing, and the influence of special interest groups can compromise the integrity of elections and erode public trust. Moreover, democratic innovations, such as ranked-choice voting and citizen assemblies, present both opportunities and challenges as societies seek to enhance democratic processes and participation.

5. Social and Economic Inequalities

Persistent social and economic inequalities pose significant challenges to democratic nations. When a significant portion of the population feels marginalized or excluded from the benefits of democracy, it can fuel social unrest, political polarization, and a loss of faith in democratic systems. Addressing inequalities, promoting social mobility, and ensuring inclusive economic policies are crucial for maintaining a healthy democratic society.

6. Environmental Challenges and Sustainable Governance

The 21st century brings pressing environmental challenges that democratic nations must address. Climate change, resource depletion, and environmental degradation require coordinated global efforts and sustainable governance. The ability of democratic systems to navigate complex environmental issues, balance economic growth with environmental sustainability, and secure intergenerational equity presents a critical challenge in the coming years.

7. Technological Advances and Cybersecurity Threats

Advancements in technology bring both opportunities and challenges to democratic nations. While digital platforms have expanded access to information and facilitated citizen engagement, they have also created vulnerabilities in the form of cybersecurity threats, election interference, and the spread of disinformation. Balancing the benefits of technology with safeguarding democratic processes and protecting individuals' privacy presents an ongoing challenge.

Conclusion

The challenges faced by democratic nations in the 21st century highlight the dynamic nature of democracy and the need for constant vigilance and adaptation. By recognizing and addressing challenges such as populism, polarization, threats to media freedom, electoral reforms, inequalities, environmental issues, and cybersecurity threats, democratic societies can work towards a more robust and inclusive democratic system. Overcoming these challenges requires the engagement and commitment of citizens, policymakers, and civil society to ensure the continued vitality of democracy in action.

Chapter 1: United States
Overview of the U.S. Political System

The United States is renowned for its democratic system, which combines elements of federalism, separation of powers, and representative democracy. In this chapter, we will provide a comprehensive overview of the U.S. political system, exploring its foundational principles, key institutions, and the interplay between branches of government. Understanding the structure and dynamics of the U.S. political system is essential for comprehending its unique democratic processes and the challenges it faces.

1. Foundational Principles of the U.S. Political System

The U.S. political system is built upon a set of foundational principles that guide its governance. These principles include popular sovereignty, limited government, individual rights, federalism, and the rule of law. We will explore how these principles shape the structure and functioning of the U.S. political system, ensuring a balance of power and protecting individual liberties.

2. The Constitution and the Three Branches of Government

The U.S. Constitution serves as the supreme law of the land, establishing the framework for the federal government and its relationship with the states. We will delve into the

Constitution's creation, its key provisions, and the system of checks and balances that ensures no single branch of government becomes too powerful. The three branches of government—legislative, executive, and judicial—will be examined in detail, highlighting their roles, responsibilities, and interdependencies.

3. The Legislative Branch: Congress

Congress, consisting of the Senate and the House of Representatives, is responsible for making laws and representing the interests of the American people. We will explore the composition and functions of Congress, including the legislative process, the role of committees, and the dynamics of party politics. Additionally, we will examine the unique features of bicameralism and the challenges faced by Congress in fulfilling its legislative duties.

4. The Executive Branch: The Presidency

The Presidency is a pivotal institution in the U.S. political system, responsible for executing and enforcing laws, conducting foreign policy, and serving as the head of state. We will delve into the powers and responsibilities of the President, the electoral process, the executive bureaucracy, and the role of the Vice President. The dynamics of presidential leadership, the limits on executive power, and the challenges faced by the Presidency will also be explored.

5. The Judicial Branch: The Supreme Court

The Supreme Court is the highest judicial authority in the United States, entrusted with interpreting the Constitution and ensuring the constitutionality of laws. We will examine the structure of the federal judiciary, the appointment and confirmation process of Supreme Court justices, and the impact of landmark Supreme Court decisions on American society. The role of judicial review, the Court's influence on policy, and the challenges of maintaining judicial independence will be discussed.

6. Federalism and the Division of Powers

The U.S. political system is characterized by federalism, a system that divides powers between the federal government and the states. We will explore the distribution of powers, the supremacy clause, and the relationship between federal and state governments. The dynamics of intergovernmental relations, debates over states' rights, and the challenges of coordinating policies in a federal system will be examined.

7. Political Parties and Elections

Political parties play a significant role in the U.S. political system, shaping public opinion, mobilizing voters, and influencing policy decisions. We will discuss the two-party system, the Democratic and Republican parties, their ideologies, and the role of third parties. The electoral process, campaign finance, voter participation, and the challenges of ensuring fair and inclusive elections will also be explored.

Conclusion

The U.S. political system, with its unique blend of federalism, separation of powers, and representative democracy, has shaped American governance for centuries. Understanding the overview of the U.S. political system provides insights into its strengths, complexities, and challenges. By examining the foundational principles, the role of key institutions, and the dynamics of political processes, we can better appreciate the intricacies of democracy in action in the United States.

Presidential vs. Parliamentary Systems

The United States has a unique political system characterized by a presidential form of government. In this chapter, we will explore the features and dynamics of the presidential system, comparing it to parliamentary systems found in other Western democracies. By examining the advantages, challenges, and implications of each system, we can gain a deeper understanding of the U.S. political system and its distinct approach to governance.

1. Presidential Systems: The U.S. Model

The U.S. presidential system is based on the principle of separation of powers, where the executive branch is separate from the legislative branch. We will delve into the features of the U.S. presidential system, including the direct election of the President, the fixed terms of office, and the extensive powers vested in the executive. The concept of the presidency as a symbol of national unity and the challenges associated with divided government will also be discussed.

2. Parliamentary Systems: Foundations and Principles

Parliamentary systems, prevalent in countries such as the United Kingdom, Germany, and France, operate on a different set of principles. We will examine the foundations of parliamentary systems, including the fusion of executive and legislative powers, the role of the prime minister, and the concept of collective responsibility. The emphasis on party discipline, the formation of coalition governments, and the advantages of proportional representation will be explored.

3. Executive-Legislative Relations: Collaboration and Accountability

A fundamental difference between presidential and parliamentary systems lies in the nature of executive-legislative relations. We will compare the mechanisms of collaboration and accountability in both systems. In a presidential system, we will explore the concept of checks and balances, the role of veto power, and the challenges of achieving policy consensus. In a parliamentary system, we will examine the importance of majority support, no-confidence votes, and the ability to pass legislation more efficiently.

4. Leadership and Stability: Presidential vs. Parliamentary Approaches

The choice between a presidential or parliamentary system can have implications for leadership and stability. We will analyze the advantages and challenges of each system in terms of leadership selection, tenure, and the ability to weather political crises. The influence of popular support, party discipline, and the impact of mid-term elections on stability and policy continuity will be discussed.

5. Representation and Accountability: The Role of Political Parties

Political parties play a crucial role in both presidential and parliamentary systems. We will examine how parties operate within each system, including their roles in candidate selection, policy formation, and maintaining party cohesion. The challenges of coalition-building in parliamentary systems and the impact of third-party dynamics on representation and policy outcomes will be explored. Additionally, we will analyze how parties contribute to accountability mechanisms in both systems.

6. Adaptability and Flexibility: Presidential and Parliamentary Reform

Both presidential and parliamentary systems have undergone reforms over time to address evolving political landscapes. We will examine reform efforts in the United States and other Western democracies, including debates on electoral reforms, campaign finance regulations, and the impact of party system dynamics. The ability of each system to adapt to changing societal needs and address democratic challenges will be evaluated.

7. Comparative Case Studies: United States, United Kingdom, Germany, and France

To provide a comprehensive analysis, we will conduct comparative case studies of the United States, the United Kingdom, Germany, and France. By examining the unique characteristics, challenges, and achievements of each system, we can gain a broader perspective on the strengths and weaknesses of presidential and parliamentary models.

Conclusion

The choice between presidential and parliamentary systems reflects the diverse approaches to democratic governance. The U.S. presidential system, with its separation of powers and emphasis on executive leadership, offers distinct advantages and challenges. By comparing it to parliamentary systems, we can appreciate the variations in executive-legislative relations, representation, accountability, and adaptability. Understanding the intricacies of presidential and parliamentary systems enhances our knowledge of democratic practices and enables us to critically evaluate their effectiveness in addressing the challenges of the 21st century.

Electoral Process and Voting Systems

The United States has a complex electoral process that plays a vital role in its democratic system. In this chapter, we will explore the intricacies of the U.S. electoral process, examining the principles, procedures, and voting systems that shape the selection of political leaders. By delving into the evolution of the electoral process and analyzing the challenges and reforms it faces, we can gain a comprehensive understanding of this crucial aspect of American democracy.

1. Principles of Democratic Elections

The foundation of democratic elections lies in the principles of universal suffrage, free and fair elections, and the right to political participation. We will explore how these principles have evolved in the United States, from the expansion of voting rights to the protection of minority representation. The concept of political equality, the role of civic education, and the importance of public confidence in the electoral process will also be discussed.

2. The Electoral College

One unique feature of the U.S. electoral process is the Electoral College, which determines the outcome of presidential elections. We will delve into the history and rationale behind the Electoral College, examining its structure, functioning, and implications for representation.

The advantages and criticisms of the Electoral College, including debates on its fairness and the potential for discrepancies between the popular vote and the electoral outcome, will be explored.

3. Primary Elections and the Nomination Process

The U.S. electoral process includes primary elections, where political parties select their candidates for general elections. We will examine the role of primary elections in shaping party platforms, mobilizing voters, and determining the candidate who will represent each party in the general election. The impact of primary elections on political polarization, the rise of independent candidates, and the challenges of maintaining a balance between party influence and popular choice will be discussed.

4. Campaign Finance and Political Advertising

Campaign finance plays a significant role in U.S. elections, with the financing of political campaigns often a topic of debate and reform. We will explore the influence of money in politics, the regulations governing campaign financing, and the role of political action committees (PACs) and Super PACs. Additionally, we will examine the impact of political advertising on voter behavior, the challenges of ensuring transparency and accountability, and the potential for undue influence.

5. Voting Systems: Plurality, Majority, and Proportional Representation

The United States utilizes a plurality voting system for most elections, but alternative voting systems exist globally. We will compare plurality, majority, and proportional representation systems, examining their advantages, challenges, and potential impact on representation and party dynamics. The role of third parties, debates on electoral reform, and the implications of different voting systems for political inclusivity and diversity will be explored.

6. Voter Registration and Access to the Ballot

Access to the ballot is a fundamental aspect of democratic elections. We will discuss the voter registration process in the United States, including debates on voter identification requirements, voter purges, and voter suppression. The challenges of ensuring equitable access to the ballot, expanding voter participation, and safeguarding against voter fraud and voter disenfranchisement will be examined.

7. Electoral Reform and Future Directions

The U.S. electoral process has undergone reforms throughout its history, driven by the need to address emerging challenges and enhance democratic practices. We will explore past and proposed reforms, including debates on campaign finance reform, redistricting, automatic voter registration, and the potential for expanding voting rights. The role of technology in the electoral process, the challenges of cybersecurity, and the potential for innovation and inclusivity in future elections will also be discussed.

Conclusion

The electoral process and voting systems are integral components of the U.S. democratic system. Understanding the principles, procedures, and challenges associated with elections in the United States allows us to critically evaluate the strengths and weaknesses of the current system. By exploring electoral reforms and considering future directions, we can envision a more inclusive and robust electoral process that upholds the principles of democracy and ensures the voices of all citizens are heard.

Political Parties and Partisan Politics

Political parties play a central role in the U.S. political system, shaping policy agendas, mobilizing voters, and influencing the dynamics of governance. In this chapter, we will explore the evolution, structure, and impact of political parties in the United States. By examining the historical development of party politics, analyzing the current landscape, and discussing the challenges and implications of partisan politics, we can gain a comprehensive understanding of their role in American democracy.

1. Historical Evolution of Political Parties

The United States has a rich history of political parties, dating back to the early years of the republic. We will delve into the historical evolution of party politics, from the Federalist and Democratic-Republican parties to the emergence of the modern two-party system. The role of third parties and their impact on American politics will also be examined, including influential moments such as the formation of the Republican Party and the rise of populist movements.

2. The Two-Party System

The United States is characterized by a two-party system, dominated by the Democratic and Republican parties. We will explore the structure, ideologies, and bases of support for each party, analyzing their platforms, electoral strategies, and the role of party elites in shaping policy agendas. The challenges faced by third parties and the potential for multi-party dynamics will also be discussed.

3. Party Organization and Functions

Political parties in the United States serve various functions beyond electoral campaigns. We will examine the internal organization of political parties, including national, state, and local party structures. The role of party leaders, committees, and grassroots activists in fundraising, candidate recruitment, and voter mobilization will be explored. Additionally, we will discuss how parties foster political participation and serve as vehicles for collective action.

4. Partisan Polarization and Ideological Divide

One of the defining features of contemporary American politics is partisan polarization and an ideological divide. We will analyze the causes and consequences of this polarization, including the role of party activists, interest groups, and media polarization. The impact of polarization on policy-making, governance, and public discourse will be examined, along with the challenges it poses to consensus-building and democratic deliberation.

5. Campaigns and Elections: Partisan Strategies

Political parties play a crucial role in campaigns and elections, mobilizing resources, and shaping electoral strategies. We will explore the dynamics of party competition, including the role of primaries, party endorsements, and campaign messaging. The influence of money in politics, the use of data analytics, and the impact of party infrastructure on electoral outcomes will also be discussed.

6. Party Platforms and Policy Agendas

Political parties articulate their policy positions through party platforms, which outline their stances on various issues. We will examine how party platforms are developed, the role of party activists and interest groups in shaping them, and the relationship between party platforms and governance. The challenges of maintaining coherence within party platforms, balancing ideological purity with electoral viability, and responding to changing societal demands will be explored.

7. Partisan Gridlock and Compromise

Partisan politics can often lead to gridlock and challenges in achieving policy consensus. We will discuss the phenomenon of partisan gridlock, examining its causes, consequences, and potential remedies. The role of party leadership, the influence of interest groups, and the impact of polarization on the ability to reach bipartisan agreements and govern effectively will be analyzed.

8. The Future of Partisan Politics

Looking ahead, we will consider the future of partisan politics in the United States. We will discuss the potential for realignment, the impact of demographic changes on party dynamics, and the potential for new issues and movements to reshape the political landscape. The role of grassroots activism, the influence of social media, and the challenges of fostering constructive partisan competition will also be examined.

Conclusion

Political parties and partisan politics are fundamental components of the U.S. political system. Understanding the historical evolution, structure, and challenges of political parties allows us to assess their impact on democratic governance and policy-making. By analyzing the dynamics of partisan politics and exploring avenues for collaboration and compromise, we can strive for a more inclusive and effective political system that serves the interests of all citizens.

Chapter 2: United Kingdom

Westminster System and Parliamentary Democracy

The United Kingdom has a rich tradition of parliamentary democracy, with the Westminster system serving as its cornerstone. In this chapter, we will explore the structure, principles, and functioning of the Westminster system, examining its historical development and its influence on British politics. By delving into the intricacies of parliamentary democracy in the United Kingdom, we can gain a comprehensive understanding of its unique features, challenges, and implications for democratic governance.

1. Origins and Evolution of the Westminster System

The Westminster system traces its roots back to the British constitutional tradition. We will delve into its origins and evolution, from the Magna Carta to the Glorious Revolution and the establishment of parliamentary sovereignty. The influence of key historical documents, such as the Bill of Rights and the Act of Union, will be examined, as well as the role of key political thinkers in shaping the principles of parliamentary democracy.

2. Structure of the Westminster System

The Westminster system is characterized by a bicameral parliament, with the House of Commons and the House of Lords playing distinct roles. We will explore the structure and composition of both houses, examining their functions, powers, and relationships. The significance of the Prime Minister, the Cabinet, and the Speaker of the House of Commons will also be discussed, along with the role of the Monarch in the parliamentary process.

3. Parliamentary Sovereignty and the Rule of Law

Central to the Westminster system is the principle of parliamentary sovereignty, which asserts that Parliament is the supreme legislative authority. We will discuss the implications of parliamentary sovereignty on the separation of powers, judicial review, and the relationship between the executive and legislative branches. The importance of the rule of law in upholding democratic principles and the challenges of balancing parliamentary sovereignty with constitutional limitations will be examined.

4. Party Politics and Parliamentary Debates

Political parties play a central role in the functioning of the Westminster system. We will explore the dynamics of party politics in the United Kingdom, including party discipline, the role of party leaders, and the impact of the party whip system. The significance of parliamentary debates, including Prime Minister's Questions and parliamentary committees, in shaping policy decisions and holding the government to account will also be discussed.

5. Electoral System and Representation

The United Kingdom employs a first-past-the-post electoral system for general elections. We will examine the characteristics of this system, including its impact on representation, political parties, and the formation of majority governments. The debates surrounding electoral reform, alternative voting systems, and the challenges of ensuring proportional representation will be explored, along with the impact of devolution on regional representation.

6. Devolution and Regional Politics

Devolution has significantly impacted the political landscape of the United Kingdom, granting varying degrees of autonomy to Scotland, Wales, and Northern Ireland. We will discuss the motivations behind devolution, the establishment of regional assemblies and parliaments, and their influence on policymaking and governance. The challenges of balancing regional autonomy with the unity of the UK, as well as the potential for further devolution and constitutional reforms, will be examined.

7. Parliamentary Committees and Scrutiny

Parliamentary committees play a crucial role in scrutinizing government actions and policies. We will explore the structure and functions of parliamentary committees, examining their role in conducting inquiries, holding hearings, and producing reports. The impact of committee scrutiny on government accountability, transparency, and the shaping of public policy will be discussed, along with the challenges faced by committees in maintaining their independence.

8. Challenges and Reform Debates

The Westminster system faces various challenges in the 21st century. We will discuss the impact of Brexit on the UK's democratic processes and the potential for constitutional reforms. The challenges of maintaining public trust in the political system, addressing regional disparities, and adapting to changing societal demands will be examined. The role of civic engagement, democratic innovations, and the potential for revitalizing the democratic process in the United Kingdom will also be explored.

Conclusion

The Westminster system and parliamentary democracy form the backbone of the United Kingdom's political system. Understanding the principles, structure, and challenges of this system allows us to critically assess its functioning and identify avenues for reform and improvement. By fostering transparency, accountability, and public participation, the United Kingdom can continue to uphold the ideals of democratic governance and respond effectively to the challenges of the 21st century.

Role of the Monarchy and Constitutional Monarchy

The United Kingdom's monarchy has played a significant role in its political system for centuries. In this chapter, we will explore the role of the monarchy and the concept of constitutional monarchy within the framework of the British political system. By delving into the historical evolution, powers, and responsibilities of the monarchy, we can gain a comprehensive understanding of its significance, challenges, and implications for democratic governance.

1. Historical Evolution of the Monarchy

The monarchy in the United Kingdom has a long and complex history. We will delve into its historical evolution, tracing its roots back to the Norman Conquest and the establishment of the monarchy's authority. The influence of key monarchs, such as King Henry VIII, Queen Elizabeth I, and Queen Victoria, on the development of the monarchy's powers and the concept of constitutional monarchy will be examined.

2. Constitutional Monarchy: Principles and Concepts

The concept of constitutional monarchy defines the relationship between the monarch, the government, and the people. We will explore the principles and concepts that underpin constitutional monarchy, including the monarch's role as a ceremonial figurehead, the separation of powers, and the importance of the rule of law. The historical developments and key constitutional documents, such as the Magna Carta and the Bill of Rights, that shaped the concept of constitutional monarchy will be discussed.

3. The Modern Monarchy: Roles and Responsibilities

In contemporary times, the monarchy's role has evolved to become primarily symbolic and ceremonial. We will examine the roles and responsibilities of the modern monarchy, including the monarch's constitutional duties, official functions, and ceremonial engagements. The significance of royal traditions, such as the State Opening of Parliament and the Queen's Speech, in the functioning of the political system will be explored.

4. Monarchy and the Constitution

The monarchy's position within the UK's unwritten constitution is a unique aspect of the British political system. We will discuss the relationship between the monarchy and the constitution, examining the monarch's role in the legislative process, the granting of royal assent, and the dissolution of Parliament. The challenges and debates surrounding the codification of the UK's constitution and the role of the monarchy within it will also be examined.

5. Influence and Soft Power

While the monarchy's powers are mostly symbolic, it retains significant influence and soft power within the political system. We will explore the ways in which the monarchy exercises its influence, including through royal prerogatives, diplomatic engagements, and public appearances. The impact of the monarchy's image, popularity, and public perception on the functioning of the political system will be discussed.

6. Monarchy and Government

The relationship between the monarchy and the government is an essential aspect of the British political system. We will examine the monarch's role in the formation of governments, including the appointment of the Prime Minister and the granting of honors. The constitutional conventions and limitations that guide the monarch's interactions with the government, such as the principle of non-interference, will be explored.

7. Debates and Challenges

The role of the monarchy within the political system is not without debates and challenges. We will discuss the debates surrounding the monarchy's funding, its tax status, and its political neutrality. The challenges of maintaining public support and relevance in a changing society will also be examined, as well as discussions on the potential future reforms and the modernization of the monarchy.

Conclusion

The monarchy and the concept of constitutional monarchy are integral parts of the United Kingdom's political system. Understanding the historical evolution, powers, and challenges of the monarchy allows us to assess its significance and its implications for democratic governance. By balancing tradition and modernity, the United Kingdom can ensure that the monarchy continues to contribute positively to its political system and maintain its relevance in the 21st century.

Devolution and Regional Politics

The United Kingdom has undergone a significant transformation in its political landscape through the process of devolution. In this chapter, we will explore the concept of devolution and its impact on regional politics within the framework of the British political system. By delving into the historical background, motivations, and consequences of devolution, we can gain a comprehensive understanding of its significance, challenges, and implications for democratic governance.

1. Historical Background of Devolution

The historical context of devolution in the United Kingdom is essential to understanding its evolution. We will explore the historical events and political movements that paved the way for devolution, including the rise of nationalism in Scotland and Wales, and the Troubles in Northern Ireland. The impact of key events such as the Scottish referendum in 1997 and the Good Friday Agreement on the devolution process will be examined.

2. Devolution Models: Scotland, Wales, and Northern Ireland

Devolution in the United Kingdom has resulted in different models of governance for Scotland, Wales, and Northern Ireland. We will examine the structures and powers of the Scottish Parliament, the Welsh Assembly, and the Northern Ireland Assembly. The motivations behind the specific devolution settlements, including demands for greater autonomy and the recognition of national identities, will be discussed.

3. Powers and Responsibilities of Devolved Governments

Devolved governments have been granted various powers and responsibilities in areas such as healthcare, education, and transportation. We will explore the extent of devolved powers in different policy domains, examining the impact of devolution on regional governance and decision-making. The challenges of coordinating policies between devolved administrations and the central UK government will also be examined.

4. Regional Identities and Nationalism

Devolution has given rise to a stronger sense of regional identity and nationalism within the United Kingdom. We will discuss the significance of regional identities, such as Scottish, Welsh, and Northern Irish, in shaping political dynamics and public opinion. The impact of nationalism on regional politics, including demands for further devolution or independence, will be examined, as well as the challenges of balancing regional aspirations with national unity.

5. Devolution and Regional Inequalities

One of the motivations behind devolution was to address regional inequalities within the United Kingdom. We will discuss the extent to which devolution has been successful in reducing disparities between regions, examining economic, social, and political indicators. The challenges of promoting inclusive growth and ensuring balanced development across different regions will be explored, as well as the potential for further policy interventions.

6. Inter-Governmental Relations and Cooperative Governance

Devolution has necessitated the establishment of inter-governmental relations and cooperative governance mechanisms. We will explore the dynamics of interactions between the central UK government and devolved administrations, including frameworks such as the Joint Ministerial Committee. The challenges and opportunities of cooperative governance in addressing shared policy issues and ensuring effective coordination will be examined.

7. Challenges and Future of Devolution

Devolution in the United Kingdom faces several challenges and uncertainties. We will discuss the challenges of managing asymmetrical devolution, including the potential for conflicts and tensions between different devolved administrations. The impact of Brexit on devolution and the potential reconfiguration of powers and responsibilities will be explored, as well as the debates surrounding the future of devolution and potential constitutional reforms.

Conclusion

Devolution has reshaped the political landscape of the United Kingdom, bringing regional politics and governance to the forefront. Understanding the motivations, structures, and challenges of devolution allows us to assess its significance and implications for democratic governance. By embracing the principles of subsidiarity, collaboration, and inclusivity, the United Kingdom can navigate the complexities of devolution and ensure that regional politics contribute positively to its democratic system.

Brexit and its Implications

Brexit, the withdrawal of the United Kingdom from the European Union, has been one of the most significant political events in recent history. In this chapter, we will explore the background, motivations, and consequences of Brexit, focusing on its implications for the United Kingdom's political system, economy, and global position. By delving into the complexities and challenges of Brexit, we can gain a comprehensive understanding of its significance and the ongoing debates surrounding its impact on democratic governance.

1. Historical Background and Factors Leading to Brexit

To understand the origins of Brexit, we will examine the historical background and the factors that contributed to the decision to leave the European Union. We will discuss the historical tensions between the United Kingdom and the EU, the role of the Conservative Party's internal dynamics, the rise of Euroscepticism, and the political landscape leading up to the 2016 referendum. The key arguments for and against Brexit, including sovereignty, immigration, and economic considerations, will be explored.

2. The Brexit Process: Negotiations and Withdrawal Agreement

We will delve into the intricacies of the Brexit process, including the negotiations between the United Kingdom and the European Union. We will discuss the key milestones, such as triggering Article 50, the negotiation of the Withdrawal Agreement, and the challenges faced by both sides. The complexities of issues such as the Irish border, trade arrangements, and the rights of EU citizens in the UK and UK citizens in the EU will be examined.

3. Implications for the United Kingdom's Political System

Brexit has had profound implications for the United Kingdom's political system. We will discuss the impact on party politics, including divisions within political parties and the rise of new political forces. The challenges of parliamentary sovereignty, the role of referendums in decision-making, and the potential reconfiguration of devolved powers will be examined. The implications for democratic accountability, constitutional reform, and the future of the UK's union will also be explored.

4. Economic Consequences and Trade Relations

Brexit has had significant economic implications for the United Kingdom. We will examine the consequences for trade relations, including the transition period and the negotiation of future trade agreements. The impact on sectors such as finance, manufacturing, agriculture, and services will be discussed. The challenges of regulatory alignment, customs arrangements, and the potential for economic divergence within the UK will be explored.

5. Global Position and International Relations

Brexit has reshaped the United Kingdom's global position and its relationships with other countries and international organizations. We will discuss the implications for the UK's influence in global governance, its diplomatic relations, and its role in international cooperation. The challenges and opportunities of forging new trade relationships, redefining the UK's global identity, and managing relations with the EU and other global powers will be examined.

6. Social and Cultural Implications

Brexit has also had social and cultural implications for the United Kingdom. We will explore the impact on issues such as immigration, identity politics, and societal divisions. The challenges of promoting social cohesion, addressing the concerns of different communities, and nurturing a sense of national unity will be examined. The role of media, public discourse, and public opinion in shaping the social and cultural dynamics surrounding Brexit will also be discussed.

7. Future Debates and Uncertainties

Brexit continues to generate debates and uncertainties about the future of the United Kingdom. We will discuss the ongoing discussions surrounding issues such as the Northern Ireland protocol, the potential for further referendums on Scottish independence, and the future relationship between the UK and the EU. The challenges of implementing and managing the changes brought about by Brexit, as well as the potential for constitutional reforms and democratic renewal, will be explored.

Conclusion

Brexit has had far-reaching implications for the United Kingdom, impacting its political system, economy, and global position. Understanding the historical context, complexities, and consequences of Brexit allows us to assess its significance for democratic governance and the challenges it presents. As the United Kingdom navigates the post-Brexit landscape, it will need to address the social, economic, and political complexities while seeking to forge new relationships and redefine its place in the world.

Chapter 3: Germany

Federal Republic and Consensus Politics

Germany, as a federal republic, has a unique political system characterized by consensus politics. In this chapter, we will explore the foundations and functioning of the German federal system, examining the principles of cooperative federalism, the distribution of powers, and the role of political parties in promoting consensus. By delving into the intricacies of German governance, we can gain a comprehensive understanding of the significance of consensus politics and its impact on democratic decision-making.

1. Historical Background of the Federal Republic

To understand the development of the federal system in Germany, we will examine the historical background, including the aftermath of World War II and the division of Germany. We will discuss the establishment of the Federal Republic of Germany (FRG) in West Germany and the German Democratic Republic (GDR) in East Germany. The reunification process and the challenges of integrating the former GDR into the federal system will also be explored.

2. The Structure of the German Federal System

We will delve into the structure of the German federal system, including the division of powers between the federal government and the 16 states (Länder). We will discuss the principles of cooperative federalism, the competencies of the federal and state governments, and the mechanisms for coordination and cooperation between them. The role of the Bundesrat, the legislative body representing the states, in the decision-making process will be examined.

3. Consensus Politics and Coalition Governments

Consensus politics is a key feature of the German political system, where coalition governments are the norm. We will explore the electoral system and party dynamics that contribute to the formation of coalition governments. The role of political parties in promoting consensus and the challenges of coalition building and maintaining stability will be discussed. The impact of consensus politics on policy-making, compromise, and representation will also be examined.

4. Electoral Reforms and Proportional Representation

The German electoral system, based on proportional representation, plays a crucial role in shaping the political landscape and facilitating consensus politics. We will discuss the electoral reforms implemented in Germany, including the threshold for parliamentary representation and the allocation of seats. The impact of the electoral system on party competition, the representation of diverse political ideologies, and the formation of coalition governments will be explored.

5. Impact of Historical Legacies on German Politics

Germany's political landscape has been influenced by its historical legacies. We will examine the impact of historical events, such as World War II and the division of Germany, on the development of the federal system and consensus politics. The challenges and opportunities of dealing with the past, including the process of Vergangenheitsbewältigung (coming to terms with the past), will be discussed. The role of historical memory and collective identity in shaping political discourse and decision-making will also be explored.

6. Social Partnership and Stakeholder Engagement

Consensus politics in Germany extends beyond political parties to encompass social partnership and stakeholder engagement. We will discuss the role of trade unions, employers' associations, and civil society organizations in shaping policy-making and promoting social dialogue. The challenges and benefits of involving various stakeholders in decision-making processes will be examined, as well as the impact of social partnership on democratic governance.

7. Challenges to Consensus Politics

Consensus politics in Germany faces several challenges in the 21st century. We will discuss the impact of political polarization, the rise of populist movements, and the fragmentation of the party system on consensus-building. The challenges of addressing social and economic disparities between regions and demographic groups will be explored, as well as the implications of societal changes, such as immigration and globalization, on consensus politics.

Conclusion

The federal system and consensus politics are fundamental elements of the German political system, shaping democratic governance and decision-making processes. Understanding the historical, structural, and cultural factors that underpin consensus politics in Germany provides valuable insights into the challenges and strengths of the system. As Germany continues to navigate the complexities of the 21st century, it will need to address the evolving societal, economic, and political dynamics while preserving the principles of consensus and cooperative federalism.

Coalition Governments and Multi-party System

Germany's political landscape is characterized by coalition governments and a vibrant multi-party system. In this chapter, we will explore the dynamics and challenges of coalition politics, examining the formation of coalition governments, the role of political parties, and the impact on democratic governance. By delving into the intricacies of coalition governments and the multi-party system in Germany, we can gain a comprehensive understanding of their significance and the complexities they present.

1. Historical Context: The Emergence of a Multi-party System

To understand the development of the multi-party system in Germany, we will examine the historical context, including the post-World War II era and the establishment of the Federal Republic of Germany. We will discuss the formation of political parties, their ideological foundations, and their role in shaping democratic governance. The impact of historical events, such as the division and reunification of Germany, on the party landscape will also be explored.

2. Electoral System and Party Landscape

We will delve into the German electoral system and its impact on the party landscape. The proportional representation system and the threshold for parliamentary representation will be discussed. We will explore the main political parties in Germany, including the Christian Democratic Union (CDU), the Social Democratic Party (SPD), the Free Democratic Party (FDP), and the Green Party, examining their ideologies, support bases, and electoral strategies. The rise of new parties, such as the Alternative for Germany (AfD), will also be explored.

3. Formation and Challenges of Coalition Governments

Coalition governments are a common feature of the German political system. We will discuss the process of coalition formation, including pre- and post-election negotiations, policy agreements, and the distribution of ministerial positions. The challenges of building and maintaining stable coalitions, such as reconciling diverse policy priorities, managing party dynamics, and preserving party cohesion, will be examined. The role of party leaders and negotiation tactics in coalition-building will also be explored.

4. Impact on Policy-making and Consensus-building

Coalition governments have a significant impact on policy-making and consensus-building in Germany. We will discuss the influence of coalition agreements on policy formulation, the need for compromise and consensus among coalition partners, and the role of the opposition in the legislative process. The challenges of balancing party interests with the pursuit of common policy objectives will be examined. The role of coalition agreements in promoting stability and accountability will also be explored.

5. Coalition Variations: From Grand Coalitions to Jamaica Coalitions

Germany has experienced various types of coalition governments, ranging from grand coalitions to more ideologically diverse coalitions, such as Jamaica coalitions. We will discuss the characteristics, advantages, and challenges of different coalition configurations. The dynamics of grand coalitions between the CDU and the SPD, as well as the potential for Jamaica coalitions involving the CDU/CSU, FDP, and Green Party, will be explored. The impact of coalition variations on policy outcomes and political dynamics will be examined.

6. Challenges and Criticisms of Coalition Governments

Coalition governments in Germany face several challenges and criticisms. We will discuss the impact of party fragmentation, the rise of populist movements, and the difficulty of consensus-building in a multi-party system. The challenges of maintaining stability, managing conflicting policy priorities, and addressing societal demands will be examined. The criticisms of coalition politics, including the perception of compromise leading to diluted policies and the potential for policy gridlock, will also be explored.

7. Future Trends and Prospects for Coalition Politics

Looking ahead, we will discuss future trends and prospects for coalition politics in Germany. We will examine the potential for shifts in party dynamics, the emergence of new political forces, and the impact of societal changes on coalition-building. The challenges and opportunities presented by issues such as climate change, migration, and social inequality will be explored. The role of coalition politics in shaping democratic governance in a rapidly changing world will be discussed.

Conclusion

Coalition governments and the multi-party system play a crucial role in shaping democratic governance in Germany. Understanding the dynamics and challenges of coalition politics provides valuable insights into the functioning of the German political system. As Germany faces the complexities of the 21st century, it will need to navigate the intricacies of coalition-building, foster consensus, and address societal demands to ensure effective and responsive democratic governance.

Electoral Reforms and Proportional Representation

Germany's electoral system is based on proportional representation, which has significant implications for the country's political landscape and democratic governance. In this chapter, we will explore the historical evolution of electoral reforms in Germany, the principles and mechanics of proportional representation, and the impact of the electoral system on party politics, representation, and democratic legitimacy. By delving into the intricacies of electoral reforms and proportional representation in Germany, we can gain a comprehensive understanding of their significance and the challenges they present.

1. Historical Background of Electoral Reforms

To understand the development of Germany's electoral system, we will examine the historical background and key milestones in electoral reforms. We will discuss the electoral systems in place during different periods, including the Weimar Republic, the Nazi era, and the post-World War II period. The influence of historical events, such as the need for stable governance and the desire to prevent the concentration of power, on electoral reforms will be explored.

2. Principles of Proportional Representation

We will delve into the principles and mechanics of proportional representation in Germany. We will discuss the concept of proportionality, which aims to ensure that the distribution of seats in parliament reflects the share of votes received by each political party. The calculation methods used, such as the Sainte-Laguë method, the Hare-Niemeyer method, and the Droop quota, will be examined. The impact of threshold requirements, such as the 5% threshold, on party representation will also be explored.

3. Electoral System and Party Dynamics

The German electoral system has a profound impact on party dynamics and the party landscape. We will discuss the incentives and strategies employed by political parties to maximize their electoral success under proportional representation. The formation of party lists, candidate selection processes, and campaign strategies will be examined. The influence of the electoral system on party competition, coalition-building, and the representation of diverse political ideologies will be explored.

4. Coalition Politics and Proportional Representation

Proportional representation facilitates coalition politics in Germany. We will discuss how the electoral system encourages party cooperation and coalition-building. The formation of coalition governments, the negotiation processes, and the distribution of power among coalition partners will be explored. The impact of proportional representation on policy outcomes, compromise, and stability in coalition governments will also be examined.

5. Representation and Democratic Legitimacy

Proportional representation is often considered to enhance representation and democratic legitimacy. We will discuss the extent to which the electoral system ensures fair representation of different political opinions, diverse social groups, and regional interests. The challenges of balancing proportionality with the need for stable governance and effective decision-making will be examined. The impact of the electoral system on the relationship between elected representatives and constituents will also be explored.

6. Criticisms and Debates on Proportional Representation

Proportional representation is not without criticisms and debates. We will examine the various criticisms leveled against the electoral system, such as the potential for fragmentation, the difficulty of forming stable governments, and the dilution of policy outcomes. The debates on potential reforms, including the introduction of majoritarian elements or hybrid systems, will be discussed. The trade-offs between proportionality and governability in electoral design will be examined.

7. International Perspectives and Comparative Analysis

We will provide international perspectives on proportional representation by examining electoral systems in other countries. A comparative analysis of different electoral systems, such as first-past-the-post, mixed-member proportional, and single transferable vote systems, will be conducted. The strengths and weaknesses of proportional representation in fostering inclusive representation, preventing majoritarian dominance, and promoting democratic accountability will be discussed.

Conclusion

Electoral reforms and the use of proportional representation have shaped Germany's political landscape and democratic governance. Understanding the principles and dynamics of the electoral system is crucial for comprehending the functioning of German democracy. As Germany faces the challenges of the 21st century, ongoing debates on electoral reforms and the continued evolution of the electoral system will play a significant role in shaping the country's democratic future.

Impact of Historical Legacies on German Politics

Germany's political landscape is deeply influenced by its historical legacies. In this chapter, we will explore the historical factors and events that have shaped German politics, examining their lasting impact on the country's democratic institutions, party system, and political culture. By delving into the intricacies of historical legacies on German politics, we can gain a comprehensive understanding of their significance and the challenges they present.

1. Historical Background: From the Holy Roman Empire to the Weimar Republic

To understand the impact of historical legacies on German politics, we will examine the historical background of the country. We will discuss the formation of the Holy Roman Empire, the influence of the Protestant Reformation, and the consolidation of territorial states. The emergence of Prussia and the unification of Germany in the 19th century will also be explored. The tumultuous period of the Weimar Republic and its collapse will be examined as a critical turning point in German history.

2. Legacy of World War II and the Nazi Era

The legacy of World War II and the Nazi era continues to shape German politics. We will discuss the profound impact of the Holocaust, the atrocities committed during the Nazi regime, and the division of Germany after the war. The process of denazification, the establishment of democratic institutions in West Germany, and the challenges of reunification will be examined. The ongoing efforts to confront and remember the past, including Holocaust remembrance and dealing with Nazi crimes, will also be explored.

3. East-West Divide and German Reunification

The division of Germany during the Cold War and the subsequent reunification have left a lasting impact on German politics. We will discuss the contrasting political systems in East and West Germany, the role of the Stasi and state surveillance in the East, and the challenges of integrating the two systems after reunification. The impact of reunification on political parties, the party system, and public sentiment in unified Germany will be explored.

4. Federalism and Regional Identities

Germany's federal structure and regional identities have their roots in historical legacies. We will discuss the influence of historical territories and regions on the formation of the federal system. The role of states (Länder) in German politics, their competencies, and their impact on policy-making will be examined. The significance of regional identities, such as Bavaria, Saxony, and Baden-Württemberg, in shaping political preferences and party dynamics will also be explored.

5. Collective Memory and Political Culture

The collective memory of historical events significantly influences German political culture. We will discuss the impact of historical legacies on notions of collective guilt, responsibility, and national identity. The importance of historical memory in shaping political attitudes, the commitment to democracy, and the rejection of extremist ideologies will be examined. The role of memorial sites, museums, and education in transmitting historical knowledge and fostering democratic values will also be explored.

6. European Integration and Germany's Role

Germany's historical legacies have shaped its approach to European integration and its role within the European Union (EU). We will discuss the impact of Germany's troubled past on its commitment to European integration, the pursuit of reconciliation with neighboring countries, and its influence within the EU. The challenges and opportunities of Germany's leadership role in Europe, including debates on austerity measures, migration, and the future of the EU, will be examined.

7. Memory Politics and Historical Debates

Memory politics and historical debates continue to shape German politics. We will explore the controversies and debates surrounding historical memory, such as the preservation of Nazi-era buildings, the handling of colonial history, and the commemoration of other historical events. The role of political parties, interest groups, and civil society organizations in shaping memory politics and historical narratives will be examined.

Conclusion

The impact of historical legacies on German politics is profound and multifaceted. Understanding the historical context and its ongoing influence is crucial for comprehending the complexities of German democracy. As Germany navigates the challenges of the 21st century, the awareness of historical legacies and their impact will be essential in shaping the country's political landscape, policy decisions, and national identity.

Chapter 4: France

Semi-Presidential System and Presidential Powers

France's political system is characterized by a unique semi-presidential system, which combines elements of both presidential and parliamentary systems. In this chapter, we will explore the intricacies of the French political system, focusing on the role and powers of the president, the relationship between the president and the prime minister, and the dynamics of governance. By delving into the complexities of the semi-presidential system and presidential powers in France, we can gain a comprehensive understanding of their significance and the challenges they present.

1. Historical Background: From Monarchy to Republic

To understand the evolution of the semi-presidential system in France, we will examine the historical background of the country. We will discuss the transition from the monarchy to the French Revolution, the establishment of the First Republic, and subsequent changes in the political system. The development of the Fifth Republic and the adoption of the semi-presidential system under Charles de Gaulle will be explored.

2. The Semi-Presidential System: Key Features and Institutions

We will delve into the key features and institutions of the semi-presidential system in France. The constitutional framework, including the role of the president, the prime minister, and the parliament, will be examined. The separation of powers, the checks and balances, and the mechanisms of accountability within the system will be explored. The influence of the French Constitution and constitutional reforms on the functioning of the semi-presidential system will also be discussed.

3. Presidential Powers: Executive Authority and Decision-Making

The president holds significant executive authority and decision-making powers in the French political system. We will discuss the extensive powers of the president, including the power to appoint the prime minister, dissolve the National Assembly, and shape foreign policy. The mechanisms of presidential decision-making, such as the Conseil des Ministres (Council of Ministers) and the use of executive orders, will be examined. The implications of strong presidential powers for democratic governance and the balance of power will also be explored.

4. President-Prime Minister Relationship: Cohabitation and Cohesion

The relationship between the president and the prime minister is a key dynamic in the semi-presidential system. We will discuss the concept of cohabitation, where the president and the prime minister belong to different political parties, and its implications for governance and policy-making. The tensions and negotiations between the president and the prime minister, the distribution of powers, and the challenges of maintaining cohesion in the executive branch will be examined.

5. Presidential Elections and Political Campaigns

Presidential elections in France are highly significant and closely followed. We will discuss the electoral process, including the two-round system and the role of political parties. The dynamics of presidential campaigns, the importance of media and public opinion, and the impact of personalities and ideologies on the electoral outcomes will be explored. The implications of presidential elections for the legitimacy and mandate of the president will also be discussed.

6. Presidentialism and Democracy: Criticisms and Debates

The semi-presidential system in France has faced criticisms and debates regarding its impact on democratic governance. We will examine the critiques of presidentialism, such as concerns about executive dominance, the concentration of power, and the potential for gridlock. The debates on potential reforms, including proposals to strengthen the role of the parliament or shift towards a parliamentary system, will be discussed. The trade-offs between presidential authority and democratic accountability will be examined.

7. International Perspectives and Comparative Analysis

We will provide international perspectives on semi-presidential systems by examining similar systems in other countries. A comparative analysis of different semi-presidential systems, such as those in Russia, Ukraine, and Taiwan, will be conducted. The similarities, differences, strengths, and weaknesses of the French semi-presidential system in ensuring effective governance and democratic representation will be explored.

Conclusion

The semi-presidential system and presidential powers in France play a crucial role in shaping the country's governance and democratic processes. Understanding the intricacies of this system, including the extensive powers of the president and the dynamics of the president-prime minister relationship, is essential for comprehending the functioning of French democracy. As France faces the challenges of the 21st century, ongoing debates on the strengths and weaknesses of the semi-presidential system will continue to shape the country's political landscape and democratic governance.

Political Ideologies and Party System

France's political landscape is characterized by a diverse range of political ideologies and a multi-party system. In this chapter, we will explore the major political ideologies in France, the historical development of the party system, and the dynamics of party politics. By delving into the complexities of political ideologies and the party system in France, we can gain a comprehensive understanding of their significance and the challenges they present.

1. Historical Background: Ideological Origins

To understand the political ideologies in France, we will examine their historical origins. We will discuss the Enlightenment and its influence on the emergence of liberal and republican ideologies. The role of the French Revolution, including the Jacobins and the Girondins, in shaping political thought and the ideological landscape will be explored. The impact of socialism, communism, and other left-wing movements on French politics will also be discussed.

2. Major Political Ideologies in France

We will explore the major political ideologies that have shaped French politics. This includes liberalism, conservatism, socialism, communism, and environmentalism, among others. We will discuss the core principles, values, and policy positions associated with each ideology. The historical development of these ideologies in France, their evolution over time, and their contemporary manifestations will be examined.

3. Party System: Historical Evolution and Party Families

The party system in France has undergone significant changes over time. We will discuss the historical evolution of the party system, including the emergence of political parties during the Third Republic and their subsequent transformations. The concept of party families, such as the left, the right, and the center, will be explored. The ideological positions, alliances, and rivalries within these party families will be examined.

4. Major Political Parties in France

We will examine the major political parties that play a significant role in French politics. This includes parties such as La République En Marche (LREM), Les Républicains (LR), the Socialist Party (PS), the National Rally (RN), and the Greens (EELV), among others. We will discuss the historical roots, ideological orientations, and policy agendas of these parties. The electoral performance, party leadership, and the challenges they face in a multi-party system will be explored.

5. Dynamics of Party Politics: Coalitions and Electoral Strategies

The dynamics of party politics in France involve the formation of coalitions and the pursuit of electoral strategies. We will discuss the patterns of coalition-building and the role of smaller parties in shaping government formation. The electoral strategies employed by political parties, including campaigning, messaging, and mobilization, will be examined. The impact of electoral systems, such as proportional representation and the two-round system, on party strategies will also be discussed.

6. Challenges and Transformations: Rise of Populism and Fragmentation

The French party system faces challenges and transformations in the 21st century. We will examine the rise of populist movements, such as the National Rally, and their impact on the traditional party landscape. The fragmentation of the party system, the decline of mainstream parties, and the emergence of new political forces will be explored. The implications of these challenges for democratic governance and political stability will be examined.

7. European and Global Context: French Political Ideologies on the World Stage

We will provide an analysis of French political ideologies in the European and global context. We will examine the positions of French political parties on European integration, globalization, and international relations. The influence of French political ideologies on European Union policies, the Franco-German relationship, and France's role in global affairs will be discussed.

Conclusion

The political ideologies and party system in France are integral to the functioning of the country's democracy. Understanding the historical development of political ideologies, the dynamics of the party system, and the challenges they face is essential for comprehending the complexities of French politics. As France confronts the challenges of the 21st century, ongoing debates on political ideologies and party politics will continue to shape the country's political landscape and democratic governance.

Electoral Laws and French Electoral Process

France's electoral system plays a crucial role in shaping its democratic governance. In this chapter, we will explore the electoral laws and the electoral process in France, focusing on the mechanisms of representation, voting systems, and the dynamics of elections. By delving into the complexities of electoral laws and the French electoral process, we can gain a comprehensive understanding of their significance and the challenges they present.

1. Historical Background: Evolution of Electoral Laws

To understand the electoral laws in France, we will examine their historical evolution. We will discuss the development of electoral laws from the French Revolution to the present day. The adoption of universal suffrage, the introduction of different voting systems, and the reforms that have shaped the French electoral process will be explored. The impact of historical events, such as the establishment of the Fifth Republic, on electoral laws will also be discussed.

2. Electoral Systems: Proportional Representation and the Two-Round System

France employs a combination of electoral systems in different elections. We will discuss the use of proportional representation in parliamentary elections and the two-round system in presidential and local elections. The principles, advantages, and disadvantages of each system will be explored. The implications of these electoral systems for political representation, party dynamics, and the formation of governments will be examined.

3. National Assembly Elections: Constituencies and Legislative Representation

National Assembly elections are of significant importance in the French electoral process. We will discuss the organization of constituencies and the allocation of seats in the National Assembly. The mechanisms of legislative representation, such as the role of political parties, candidate selection, and the party-list system, will be examined. The impact of electoral boundaries and gerrymandering on representation will also be explored.

4. Presidential Elections: Direct Voting and Runoff System

Presidential elections in France are closely watched and highly influential. We will discuss the electoral process for presidential elections, including the direct voting system and the two-round runoff system. The mechanisms of candidate nomination, campaign dynamics, and the role of political parties in presidential elections will be examined. The implications of the presidential electoral process for democratic legitimacy and the mandate of the president will also be discussed.

5. Local Elections: Decentralization and Electoral Dynamics

Local elections in France play a crucial role in decentralized governance. We will explore the electoral process for local elections, including the election of mayors and regional representatives. The mechanisms of local representation, party competition at the local level, and the impact of local elections on regional and municipal governance will be examined. The challenges and opportunities of local elections for citizen participation and local democracy will also be discussed.

6. Campaign Finance and Political Advertising

We will delve into the regulations and practices of campaign finance and political advertising in France. The laws governing campaign financing, the role of political parties, and the transparency of political donations will be examined. The use of media and political advertising in election campaigns, including debates, televised appearances, and online campaigning, will be explored. The implications of campaign finance and political advertising for democratic processes and equal opportunities in elections will be discussed.

7. Challenges and Reforms: Voter Turnout and Electoral Innovations

France faces challenges and ongoing debates regarding its electoral process. We will examine the issue of voter turnout and the efforts to increase citizen participation in elections. The role of electoral innovations, such as e-voting and voting by mail, in enhancing the electoral process will be explored. The debates on electoral reforms, including potential changes to the voting systems and campaign regulations, will be discussed. The implications of these challenges and potential reforms for democratic legitimacy and electoral fairness will be examined.

Conclusion

The electoral laws and the French electoral process are integral to the functioning of democracy in France. Understanding the mechanisms of representation, the use of different voting systems, and the dynamics of elections is essential for comprehending the complexities of the French electoral system. As France continues to navigate the challenges of the 21st century, ongoing debates on electoral laws and potential reforms will shape the country's political landscape and democratic governance.

Challenges of Immigration and Identity Politics

France, like many Western democracies, grapples with the challenges posed by immigration and identity politics. In this chapter, we will explore the complex issues surrounding immigration, integration, multiculturalism, and the politics of identity in France. By delving into these challenges, we can gain a comprehensive understanding of their significance and the implications they have for French democracy.

1. Historical Context: Immigration and Colonial Legacy

To understand the challenges of immigration in France, we will examine the historical context, including France's colonial past and its impact on immigration patterns. We will discuss the waves of immigration from former colonies, such as Algeria, Morocco, and Tunisia, and the subsequent waves from other parts of the world. The legacies of colonialism, including questions of citizenship, identity, and social integration, will be explored.

2. Immigration Policies and Debates

We will examine the immigration policies and debates in France, including the legal frameworks and regulations governing immigration. The evolution of immigration policies over time, from labor migration to family reunification and asylum, will be discussed. The challenges of balancing humanitarian concerns, national security, and social cohesion in immigration policies will be explored. The debates surrounding immigration, including public opinion, political discourse, and policy responses, will also be analyzed.

3. Integration and Multiculturalism

Integration and multiculturalism are key aspects of the immigration challenge in France. We will discuss the approaches to integration, including the policies and programs aimed at promoting social inclusion, language acquisition, and employment opportunities for immigrants. The tensions between assimilationist and multiculturalist models of integration will be explored. The debates surrounding the role of religion, cultural diversity, and the question of national identity in the integration process will also be examined.

4. Identity Politics and Secularism

Identity politics and secularism play a significant role in the immigration discourse in France. We will discuss the principles of laïcité (secularism) and its impact on religious practices and cultural expressions in the public sphere. The debates surrounding the wearing of religious symbols, such as the hijab, in public institutions and the tension between freedom of religion and secular values will be examined. The implications of identity politics for social cohesion, citizenship, and the rights of marginalized communities will also be explored.

5. Rise of Far-Right Populism and Anti-Immigration Sentiment

The rise of far-right populism and anti-immigration sentiment has had a profound impact on French politics. We will examine the emergence of far-right parties, such as the National Rally, and their electoral success. The factors contributing to anti-immigration sentiment, including economic anxieties, cultural anxieties, and fears of terrorism, will be discussed. The implications of far-right populism for democratic norms, social cohesion, and minority rights will be analyzed.

6. Social and Economic Integration Challenges

We will delve into the challenges faced by immigrants in social and economic integration. The issues of discrimination, unequal access to education, housing, and employment opportunities will be explored. The role of social policies, including education and job training programs, in promoting equal opportunities and social mobility for immigrants will be discussed. The challenges of addressing socio-economic disparities and fostering inclusive communities will also be examined.

7. Debates on Immigration Reform and Policy Responses

We will analyze the debates on immigration reform and the policy responses in France. This includes discussions on border control, asylum procedures, immigration quotas, and family reunification policies. The efforts to create a more inclusive and fair immigration system, while addressing concerns of social cohesion and national security, will be explored. The implications of immigration reform for French democracy, human rights, and global migration governance will also be discussed.

Conclusion

The challenges of immigration and identity politics pose complex issues for French democracy. Understanding the historical context, policy debates, and social dynamics surrounding immigration is crucial for addressing these challenges effectively. By promoting inclusive integration, multiculturalism, and social cohesion, France can strive towards a more inclusive and democratic society.

Chapter 5: Challenges to Democracy
Rise of Populism and its Impact on Western Democracies

In recent years, Western democracies have witnessed the rise of populist movements and leaders who challenge the established political order. In this chapter, we will explore the phenomenon of populism, its causes, characteristics, and its impact on democratic systems. By delving into the complexities of the rise of populism, we can gain a comprehensive understanding of its significance and the challenges it presents to Western democracies.

1. Defining Populism: Concept and Characteristics

To understand the rise of populism, we will begin by defining the concept and exploring its key characteristics. We will examine the common features of populist movements, such as anti-establishment rhetoric, appeals to the "people," and a rejection of traditional political elites. The relationship between populism and democracy, including its potential threats and challenges, will be discussed.

2. Historical Context: Rise of Populist Movements

We will explore the historical context that has contributed to the rise of populist movements in Western democracies. This will include an examination of socio-economic factors, such as globalization, economic inequality, and the erosion of the middle class. We will also discuss the impact of cultural and identity issues, including immigration, nationalism, and the backlash against multiculturalism. The historical roots of populist movements, from past movements to contemporary iterations, will be analyzed.

3. Populist Leaders and their Appeal

We will analyze the figureheads of populist movements and their appeal to the electorate. This includes examining the leadership styles, communication strategies, and policy agendas of prominent populist leaders. We will discuss how populist leaders tap into popular grievances, exploit anti-establishment sentiment, and offer simple solutions to complex problems. The charismatic appeal of populist leaders and their ability to resonate with specific voter groups will be explored.

4. Populism and Electoral Politics

The impact of populism on electoral politics in Western democracies will be examined. We will discuss how populist movements and leaders disrupt traditional party systems, challenge mainstream political parties, and reshape electoral dynamics. The role of populism in influencing election outcomes, coalition formations, and party realignment will be explored. The implications of populist electoral successes for democratic representation and governance will be analyzed.

5. Populism and Political Polarization

We will explore the relationship between populism and political polarization. Populist movements often thrive in polarized political environments, where divisions between "us" and "them" are emphasized. We will discuss how populist rhetoric exacerbates existing divisions, fuels social and political polarization, and hampers constructive dialogue and compromise. The challenges of governing in polarized contexts and the potential threats to democratic institutions will be examined.

6. Populism and the Media

The role of media in the rise of populism and its impact on democratic processes will be analyzed. We will discuss how populist leaders utilize social media, online platforms, and alternative media channels to bypass traditional media gatekeepers and communicate directly with their supporters. The challenges of disinformation, echo chambers, and the erosion of trust in the media will be explored. The implications for media pluralism, freedom of the press, and the role of journalism in a populist era will be discussed.

7. Populism and Democratic Norms

We will examine the impact of populism on democratic norms and institutions. Populist leaders often challenge the independence of the judiciary, freedom of the press, and other democratic checks and balances. We will discuss the erosion of democratic norms, threats to the rule of law, and the potential consequences for democratic governance. The role of civil society organizations, democratic reforms, and international cooperation in safeguarding democratic values in the face of populism will be analyzed.

Conclusion

The rise of populism poses significant challenges to Western democracies, impacting electoral politics, political polarization, media dynamics, and democratic norms. Understanding the causes and consequences of populism is crucial for developing effective strategies to preserve and strengthen democratic systems in the face of these challenges.

Political Polarization and Gridlock

Political polarization and gridlock have become defining features of contemporary democracies, posing significant challenges to effective governance and democratic decision-making. In this chapter, we will explore the causes, consequences, and implications of political polarization and gridlock in Western democracies. By delving into the complexities of this challenge, we can gain a comprehensive understanding of its significance and explore potential strategies for overcoming polarization and fostering constructive governance.

1. Understanding Political Polarization

We will begin by defining political polarization and examining its manifestations in Western democracies. Political polarization refers to the deep ideological and partisan divisions that exist within society and political institutions. We will explore the factors contributing to political polarization, such as socio-economic disparities, cultural differences, identity politics, and media fragmentation. The impact of polarization on public discourse, trust in institutions, and democratic legitimacy will be analyzed.

2. Causes of Political Polarization

We will delve into the causes of political polarization, considering both structural and contextual factors. Structural factors include changes in the media landscape, the influence of social media and echo chambers, and the role of interest groups and party activists. Contextual factors encompass issues such as economic inequality, immigration, cultural clashes, and the politicization of social and moral values. By understanding these underlying causes, we can better grasp the roots of political polarization.

3. Consequences of Political Polarization

We will examine the consequences of political polarization on democratic systems and governance. Polarization often leads to increased ideological rigidity, a decline in bipartisan cooperation, and the erosion of compromise and consensus-building. This can result in gridlock in legislative bodies, policy paralysis, and a lack of responsiveness to public needs. The implications of polarization for democratic representation, public trust, and the capacity to address pressing challenges will be discussed.

4. Media and Political Polarization

The role of media in exacerbating political polarization will be explored. We will discuss the influence of partisan media outlets, the rise of echo chambers, and the spread of misinformation and disinformation. The impact of social media platforms, filter bubbles, and algorithmic bias on shaping public opinion and reinforcing partisan divides will be analyzed. Strategies for promoting media literacy, fostering diverse media ecosystems, and mitigating the negative effects of media polarization will be examined.

5. Partisan Gerrymandering and Electoral Systems

We will examine how partisan gerrymandering and electoral systems can contribute to political polarization. The manipulation of electoral boundaries to favor one political party can lead to the entrenchment of polarized districts and the marginalization of moderate voices. We will discuss the implications of gerrymandering for electoral competition, representation, and the prospects for bridging ideological divides. Alternative electoral systems that promote greater proportionality and inclusiveness will also be explored.

6. Overcoming Political Polarization

Strategies for overcoming political polarization and fostering constructive governance will be discussed. This includes promoting dialogue and civil discourse, encouraging cross-party collaboration, and finding common ground on key policy issues. We will explore the role of leadership in bridging divides and fostering a sense of national unity. The importance of civic education, deliberative democracy, and grassroots movements in mitigating polarization will also be examined.

7. Institutional Reforms and Deliberative Processes

We will analyze institutional reforms and deliberative processes that can help address political polarization. This includes reforms to the legislative process, such as filibuster reform, to encourage greater deliberation and compromise. We will discuss the role of independent redistricting commissions in promoting fair electoral boundaries. The potential of participatory democracy, citizen assemblies, and deliberative polling to foster inclusive decision-making and bridge partisan divides will be explored.

Conclusion

Political polarization and gridlock pose significant challenges to the functioning and legitimacy of democratic systems. Overcoming polarization requires concerted efforts at various levels, from individual citizens to political leaders and institutions. By understanding the causes and consequences of polarization, and exploring strategies for fostering constructive governance, we can work towards a more inclusive, responsive, and resilient democratic future.

Threats to Freedom of Press and Media

Freedom of the press and media play a vital role in upholding democratic principles by ensuring transparency, accountability, and the free flow of information. However, in recent years, Western democracies have faced significant challenges to press freedom. In this chapter, we will explore the various threats to freedom of the press and media and their implications for democratic societies. By understanding these challenges, we can assess their impact on democratic processes and explore potential solutions to safeguard and promote a free and independent media.

1. The Importance of a Free and Independent Press

We will begin by emphasizing the fundamental importance of a free and independent press in democratic societies. The role of the media in providing citizens with accurate and diverse information, serving as a watchdog on power, and fostering public discourse will be examined. We will explore the historical and philosophical underpinnings of press freedom and its role in democratic governance.

2. Attacks on Journalists and Press Freedom

We will examine the alarming rise in attacks on journalists and the implications for freedom of the press. This includes physical assaults, harassment, and even killings of journalists in various parts of the world. The chapter will highlight specific cases and examples to illustrate the gravity of the situation and the challenges faced by journalists in carrying out their critical role.

3. Legal and Regulatory Challenges

We will explore legal and regulatory challenges that pose threats to press freedom. This includes laws that restrict journalists' ability to investigate and report on critical issues, such as national security, corruption, or human rights abuses. We will examine defamation laws, anti-terrorism legislation, and other measures that can be misused to silence dissenting voices and curtail press freedom.

4. Political Interference and Media Capture

Political interference in media operations and the phenomenon of media capture will be discussed. We will explore instances where governments or powerful individuals seek to control or manipulate media outlets for political or economic gain. The chapter will delve into the implications of media capture on media plurality, diversity, and the public's access to unbiased and independent information.

5. Economic Pressures and Media Ownership

The impact of economic pressures and media ownership concentration on press freedom will be examined. We will discuss the challenges posed by media consolidation, the decline of traditional revenue models, and the rise of digital platforms. The influence of advertising, corporate interests, and market forces on journalistic independence and the diversity of media voices will be analyzed.

6. Disinformation, Misinformation, and the Spread of Fake News

We will explore the challenges posed by disinformation, misinformation, and the spread of fake news in the digital age. The chapter will examine the manipulation of information through social media platforms, the role of bots and trolls in shaping public opinion, and the erosion of trust in traditional news sources. The implications of these phenomena for democratic processes, public discourse, and informed decision-making will be discussed.

7. Promoting and Safeguarding Press Freedom

Strategies for promoting and safeguarding press freedom will be explored. This includes advocating for legal protections, defending journalists' rights, and fostering international cooperation to address cross-border challenges. We will discuss the role of media literacy, fact-checking initiatives, and responsible journalism in countering disinformation. The importance of supporting independent media organizations, ensuring media plurality, and promoting ethical journalism will also be emphasized.

Conclusion

Threats to freedom of the press and media pose significant challenges to democratic societies. Safeguarding press freedom requires a multi-faceted approach, encompassing legal protections, international solidarity, and efforts to promote media literacy and responsible journalism. By addressing these challenges, we can protect the integrity of democratic processes and ensure that the media continues to serve as a cornerstone of democratic accountability and transparency.

Electoral Reform Debates and Democratic Innovations

Democratic societies continually grapple with the need for electoral reforms and innovative approaches to strengthen the democratic process. In this chapter, we will explore the debates surrounding electoral reform and the introduction of democratic innovations. By examining the motivations, proposals, and potential implications of these reforms, we can gain insights into how Western democracies are adapting to contemporary challenges and striving to enhance democratic participation and representation.

1. The Need for Electoral Reform

We will begin by examining the rationale behind electoral reform and the challenges that prompt the need for change. This includes issues such as low voter turnout, the lack of diversity in political representation, and concerns about the influence of money in politics. We will explore how these challenges impact the legitimacy and effectiveness of democratic systems, and why electoral reform is seen as a potential solution.

2. Proportional Representation vs. Majoritarian Systems

The chapter will delve into the debate between proportional representation (PR) and majoritarian systems, which are two prominent models used in Western democracies. We will explore the strengths and weaknesses of each system, including their impact on political representation, party dynamics, and the ability to accommodate diverse voices and viewpoints. Case studies of countries employing different electoral systems will be examined to provide a comparative analysis.

3. Alternative Voting Methods

We will explore alternative voting methods that are gaining attention as potential democratic innovations. This includes ranked-choice voting, where voters rank candidates in order of preference, and mixed-member proportional systems, which combine elements of PR and majoritarian systems. We will analyze the potential benefits and challenges associated with these alternative methods and discuss their implications for representation, accountability, and the formation of government.

4. Campaign Finance Reform

The influence of money in politics and the need for campaign finance reform will be discussed. We will examine the challenges posed by the increasing cost of political campaigns, the role of wealthy donors and special interest groups, and the potential impact on the fairness and integrity of the electoral process. The chapter will explore various approaches to campaign finance reform, including public financing, stricter regulations, and transparency measures.

5. Voting Rights and Access

The chapter will address the ongoing debates surrounding voting rights and access. We will explore the challenges faced by marginalized communities, including voter suppression, restrictive identification requirements, and gerrymandering. The discussion will include efforts to enhance access to the voting booth through initiatives such as early voting, automatic voter registration, and the expansion of mail-in and online voting.

6. Democratic Innovations and Citizen Engagement

We will explore the concept of democratic innovations and their role in enhancing citizen engagement and participation. This includes initiatives such as citizen assemblies, deliberative polling, and participatory budgeting, which seek to involve citizens directly in decision-making processes. We will examine case studies where these innovations have been implemented and assess their impact on democratic legitimacy, trust, and policy outcomes.

7. Evaluating the Impacts of Electoral Reforms

The chapter will critically evaluate the impacts of electoral reforms and democratic innovations. We will examine empirical evidence, case studies, and expert opinions to assess the effectiveness of various reforms in addressing the challenges to democracy. The discussion will include considerations of representation, inclusivity, political stability, and the broader goals of democratic governance.

Conclusion

Electoral reform debates and democratic innovations play a crucial role in shaping the future of Western democracies. By addressing the challenges of representation, political participation, and accountability, these reforms strive to strengthen the democratic process and ensure that it remains responsive and inclusive. Through ongoing discussions, evaluations, and experimentation, societies can continue to adapt their electoral systems and democratic practices to meet the evolving needs and aspirations of their citizens.

Chapter 6: Democratic Institutions and Civil Society
Role of Judiciary and Rule of Law

The judiciary and the rule of law are fundamental pillars of democratic societies. In this chapter, we will explore the crucial role played by the judiciary in upholding the rule of law, ensuring justice, and safeguarding democratic principles. By examining the independence, accountability, and functions of the judiciary, we can gain a deeper understanding of its significance within Western democracies.

1. The Importance of an Independent Judiciary

We will begin by highlighting the importance of an independent judiciary in democratic systems. We will explore the principles and values that underpin judicial independence, such as impartiality, fairness, and freedom from external influences. Through case studies and examples, we will analyze the impact of an independent judiciary on democratic governance, the protection of individual rights, and the separation of powers.

2. Judicial Review and Constitutional Interpretation

The chapter will delve into the concept of judicial review and the role of the judiciary in interpreting and upholding constitutions. We will examine landmark cases where the judiciary has played a significant role in shaping constitutional interpretation and establishing legal precedents. The discussion will include the balance between judicial activism and judicial restraint, as well as the implications for democratic governance.

3. Checks and Balances

We will explore the concept of checks and balances and the role of the judiciary within this system. We will examine how the judiciary acts as a check on the executive and legislative branches, ensuring accountability, preventing abuse of power, and safeguarding individual rights. The discussion will also address the potential tensions and challenges that arise from the exercise of judicial power.

4. Judicial Independence and Accountability

While judicial independence is vital, the judiciary is not immune to the need for accountability. This section will discuss mechanisms for ensuring accountability within the judiciary, including codes of conduct, judicial disciplinary processes, and judicial review of judicial decisions. We will explore the delicate balance between independence and accountability and the implications for democratic governance and public trust.

5. Access to Justice and Judicial Reform

The chapter will address the issue of access to justice and the importance of a fair and accessible judicial system.

We will examine the challenges faced by marginalized groups in accessing justice and the efforts made to enhance access through legal aid, alternative dispute resolution mechanisms, and court reforms. The discussion will also include the role of technology in improving access to justice and the potential risks and benefits associated with digitalization.

6. International Law and Human Rights

We will explore the role of the judiciary in upholding international law and protecting human rights. This section will examine how national courts interpret and apply international legal principles and treaties, including the European Convention on Human Rights and the Universal Declaration of Human Rights. The discussion will highlight the challenges and opportunities presented by the intersection of national and international law.

7. Judicial Integrity and Anti-Corruption Efforts

The chapter will address the importance of judicial integrity and the efforts to combat corruption within the judiciary. We will examine the risks and consequences of judicial corruption, as well as the measures taken to promote transparency, accountability, and ethical conduct. The discussion will include international initiatives, such as the

United Nations Convention against Corruption, and the role of civil society in monitoring judicial integrity.

Conclusion

The role of the judiciary and the rule of law in democratic societies is essential for upholding individual rights, ensuring justice, and maintaining the balance of power. By examining the principles of judicial independence, constitutional interpretation, checks and balances, and access to justice, we gain a deeper appreciation for the significance of the judiciary within democratic institutions. It is through a robust and independent judiciary that democratic societies can uphold the rule of law, protect individual freedoms, and maintain the trust and confidence of their citizens.

Checks and Balances in Western Democracies

Checks and balances are a fundamental aspect of democratic systems, ensuring the separation of powers, preventing the concentration of authority, and promoting accountability. In this chapter, we will explore the mechanisms and institutions that contribute to the system of checks and balances within Western democracies. By examining the roles and interactions of the executive, legislative, and judicial branches, as well as other accountability mechanisms, we can gain a deeper understanding of how these systems operate and their impact on democratic governance.

1. The Concept of Checks and Balances

We will begin by providing an overview of the concept of checks and balances in democratic systems. We will explain the rationale behind the establishment of checks and balances, emphasizing the importance of preventing abuses of power, ensuring accountability, and protecting individual rights. Through historical examples and comparative analysis, we will highlight the different approaches to checks and balances in Western democracies.

2. The Executive Branch and Its Limits

This section will focus on the role of the executive branch and the checks and balances placed upon it. We will examine the powers and responsibilities of the executive, such as the enforcement of laws, foreign policy, and executive orders. We will explore the mechanisms that constrain executive power, including legislative oversight, judicial review, and the role of independent agencies. Case studies will illustrate instances where the executive branch has been held accountable and the impact on democratic governance.

3. The Legislative Branch and Its Oversight

The chapter will then turn to the legislative branch and its role in checks and balances. We will discuss the functions of the legislature, such as lawmaking, budgetary control, and oversight of the executive. We will analyze the mechanisms through which the legislative branch exercises its oversight role, including committee hearings, inquiries, and impeachment processes. The discussion will also address the challenges and potential pitfalls associated with legislative oversight.

4. The Judicial Branch and Its Role in Constitutional Review

We will explore the role of the judiciary in checks and balances, with a particular focus on constitutional review. We will examine the power of the judiciary to interpret laws and the constitution, ensuring their compatibility with democratic principles. Through case studies, we will illustrate how the judiciary acts as a check on both the executive and legislative branches, protecting individual rights and upholding the rule of law.

5. Independent Oversight Institutions

In addition to the three branches of government, Western democracies often establish independent oversight institutions to enhance checks and balances. This section will explore institutions such as ombudsman offices, audit bodies, and anti-corruption commissions. We will examine their mandates, powers, and effectiveness in promoting transparency, accountability, and good governance. The discussion will also address the challenges these institutions face in maintaining independence and addressing emerging issues.

6. Civil Society and Media as Accountability Mechanisms

Civil society organizations and a free and independent media play a crucial role in providing additional checks and balances in democratic systems. We will explore the importance of a vibrant civil society, including advocacy groups, non-governmental organizations, and grassroots movements, in holding governments accountable and representing the interests of citizens. We will also examine the role of the media in exposing abuses of power, promoting transparency, and informing the public.

7. Interactions and Challenges in Checks and Balances

The chapter will analyze the interactions and potential challenges within the system of checks and balances. We will explore issues such as the potential for gridlock and the need for cooperation between branches of government. We will also address concerns regarding the politicization of oversight mechanisms and the erosion of checks and balances in times of crisis. Case studies will illustrate real-world examples of challenges and potential solutions.

Conclusion

Checks and balances are essential components of democratic systems, promoting accountability, preventing abuses of power, and safeguarding individual rights. By examining the roles and interactions of the executive, legislative, and judicial branches, as well as independent oversight institutions, civil society, and the media, we gain a comprehensive understanding of how checks and balances operate in Western democracies. It is through a robust system of checks and balances that democratic governance is strengthened, ensuring the principles of transparency, accountability, and the protection of citizens' rights.

Role of Civil Society Organizations and Interest Groups

Civil society organizations and interest groups play a crucial role in democratic systems, representing the interests of citizens, advocating for social and political change, and contributing to the overall functioning of democratic governance. In this chapter, we will delve into the significance of civil society organizations and interest groups in Western democracies. We will examine their roles, functions, challenges, and impact on policy-making and democratic participation.

1. Understanding Civil Society Organizations and Interest Groups

We will begin by providing an overview of civil society organizations and interest groups, defining their roles and distinguishing characteristics. We will explore the diverse range of organizations and groups that make up civil society, including non-governmental organizations (NGOs), community-based organizations, advocacy groups, professional associations, and trade unions. Through examples, we will highlight their different purposes, forms of engagement, and areas of focus.

2. The Importance of Civil Society in Democratic Governance

This section will focus on the significance of civil society organizations in democratic systems. We will discuss how civil society acts as a link between citizens and the government, representing diverse voices, advocating for social justice, and promoting democratic values. We will examine how civil society organizations contribute to policy-making processes, participate in public discourse, and foster democratic accountability.

3. Functions and Activities of Civil Society Organizations

We will delve into the various functions and activities carried out by civil society organizations and interest groups. This includes research and analysis, policy advocacy, public awareness campaigns, community engagement, and service provision. We will provide case studies and examples to illustrate the impact of civil society organizations in areas such as human rights, environmental protection, social welfare, and democratic reforms.

4. Challenges Faced by Civil Society Organizations

The chapter will address the challenges and constraints faced by civil society organizations and interest groups in Western democracies. This includes legal and regulatory obstacles, limited access to resources, restrictions on freedom of assembly and association, and polarization of public discourse. We will discuss the implications of these challenges on the effectiveness and sustainability of civil society organizations, as well as potential strategies to address them.

5. Civil Society and Democratic Participation

We will explore the role of civil society organizations in promoting democratic participation and citizen engagement. We will examine how these organizations facilitate public deliberation, mobilize citizens, and empower marginalized groups to participate in decision-making processes. We will also discuss the importance of inclusivity and diversity within civil society, ensuring that all voices are represented and heard.

6. Collaboration and Partnership between Civil Society and Government

The chapter will delve into the dynamics of collaboration and partnership between civil society organizations and the government. We will discuss mechanisms for engagement, such as consultations, public-private partnerships, and participatory governance initiatives. We will examine successful examples of collaboration and explore the benefits and challenges of these partnerships in promoting democratic governance.

7. Role of Interest Groups in Democratic Politics

This section will focus specifically on interest groups and their role in democratic politics. We will examine how interest groups represent specific constituencies and advocate for their policy preferences. We will discuss the different types of interest groups, their strategies for influencing policy decisions, and the potential risks associated with their influence. The discussion will also address the role of lobbying, campaign finance, and transparency in the interactions between interest groups and democratic institutions.

8. Ethical Considerations and Accountability of Civil Society Organizations

The chapter will address the ethical considerations and accountability of civil society organizations and interest groups. We will discuss issues such as transparency, accountability, conflicts of interest, and the responsible use of resources. We will explore mechanisms for self-regulation, external oversight, and the role of the media and public scrutiny in ensuring the integrity of civil society organizations.

Conclusion

Civil society organizations and interest groups are vital components of democratic governance, contributing to the pluralistic nature of Western democracies. By advocating for citizen interests, fostering public participation, and providing checks and balances on governmental power, civil society organizations and interest groups play a critical role in ensuring the functioning and responsiveness of democratic systems. Through this chapter, we aim to deepen our understanding of their roles, challenges, and impact, emphasizing the importance of a vibrant and diverse civil society in sustaining democratic values and principles.

Importance of a Free and Independent Judiciary

The judiciary is a fundamental pillar of democratic governance, playing a critical role in upholding the rule of law, protecting individual rights, and ensuring the separation of powers. In this chapter, we will delve into the significance of a free and independent judiciary in Western democracies. We will explore the key principles and functions of the judiciary, the challenges it faces, and its role in safeguarding democratic values.

1. Understanding the Role of the Judiciary

We will begin by providing an overview of the role and responsibilities of the judiciary within democratic systems. We will explore the concept of judicial independence and the importance of impartiality and fairness in delivering justice. We will discuss the different levels of the judiciary, including the Supreme Court, appellate courts, and lower courts, and their respective functions.

2. Separation of Powers and Checks and Balances

This section will focus on the interplay between the judiciary and other branches of government, highlighting the importance of the separation of powers and checks and balances. We will examine how the judiciary acts as a check on the executive and legislative branches, ensuring that they operate within the confines of the law and the constitution.

We will also discuss the implications of a harmonious relationship between the judiciary and other branches of government for democratic governance.

3. Safeguarding Individual Rights and Liberties

One of the primary functions of the judiciary is to safeguard individual rights and liberties. We will explore how the judiciary protects civil liberties, such as freedom of speech, freedom of assembly, and the right to privacy. We will discuss landmark cases and legal precedents that have shaped the protection of individual rights in Western democracies. Additionally, we will examine the challenges faced by the judiciary in balancing individual rights with societal interests and security concerns.

4. Judicial Review and Constitutional Interpretation

Judicial review is a key function of the judiciary, allowing it to assess the constitutionality of laws and government actions. We will delve into the power of judicial review and its significance in ensuring that legislative and executive actions comply with the constitution. We will discuss different approaches to constitutional interpretation, including originalism, textualism, and living constitutionalism, and their implications for democratic governance.

5. Judicial Independence and Accountability

This section will address the importance of judicial independence as a cornerstone of democratic governance. We will examine the factors that contribute to judicial independence, including the appointment and tenure of judges, financial autonomy, and safeguards against political interference. At the same time, we will explore the need for judicial accountability mechanisms to maintain public trust and confidence in the judiciary.

6. Challenges to Judicial Independence

The chapter will discuss the challenges and threats to judicial independence in Western democracies. We will examine issues such as political pressure, judicial activism, judicial misconduct, and the potential influence of interest groups and public opinion on judicial decision-making. We will also explore the impact of populist movements and authoritarian tendencies on the independence of the judiciary.

7. Judicial Ethics and Professionalism

Ethics and professionalism are vital aspects of the judiciary's functioning and credibility. We will discuss the ethical principles that judges are expected to uphold, including impartiality, integrity, and the avoidance of conflicts of interest. We will also examine the mechanisms in place to enforce judicial ethics and hold judges accountable for their conduct.

8. Judicial Reform and Modernization

This section will address the ongoing debates and efforts surrounding judicial reform and modernization. We will discuss initiatives aimed at enhancing the efficiency, accessibility, and transparency of the judiciary. We will explore topics such as the use of technology in court proceedings, alternative dispute resolution mechanisms, and the need for diversity and inclusivity within the judiciary.

Conclusion

A free and independent judiciary is a cornerstone of democratic governance, ensuring the rule of law, protecting individual rights, and upholding the principles of justice and equality. Through this chapter, we have explored the crucial role played by the judiciary in Western democracies, as well as the challenges and opportunities it faces in the 21st century. We conclude by emphasizing the importance of preserving and strengthening the independence and integrity of the judiciary to safeguard democracy for future generations.

Chapter 7: Democratic Governance in the Digital Age

Impact of Technology on Democracy and Elections

In the digital age, technology has profoundly transformed various aspects of democratic governance, including elections, political participation, and information dissemination. In this chapter, we will explore the wide-ranging impact of technology on democracy, focusing specifically on its influence on elections. We will examine the opportunities and challenges presented by technological advancements, the role of social media platforms, and the implications for democratic processes and outcomes.

1. The Digital Revolution and Democracy

We will begin by providing an overview of the digital revolution and its implications for democratic governance. We will explore how technological advancements, such as the internet, social media, and digital communication tools, have revolutionized the way citizens engage with political processes, access information, and participate in public discourse. We will also discuss the potential benefits and risks associated with the integration of technology into democratic systems.

2. Evolving Landscape of Electoral Campaigns

This section will focus on the impact of technology on electoral campaigns. We will examine how digital tools and platforms have transformed campaign strategies, voter targeting, and communication between candidates and voters. We will discuss the use of social media, online advertising, data analytics, and micro-targeting techniques, and their implications for the fairness, transparency, and effectiveness of electoral campaigns.

3. Online Voter Engagement and Mobilization

The internet and social media platforms have provided new avenues for voter engagement and mobilization. We will explore how digital platforms have facilitated online voter registration, voter education initiatives, and grassroots mobilization efforts. We will discuss the benefits of increased accessibility and participation, as well as the challenges associated with misinformation, echo chambers, and the digital divide.

4. Digital Disinformation and Election Integrity

The rise of digital platforms has also brought about concerns regarding the spread of disinformation, fake news, and election interference. We will examine the challenges posed by the proliferation of misinformation during election cycles, the manipulation of public opinion through social media, and the potential threats to the integrity of electoral processes. We will discuss the role of technology companies, government regulation, and media literacy in addressing these challenges.

5. Protecting Data Privacy and Security

As technology becomes more integrated into democratic processes, the protection of data privacy and cybersecurity becomes paramount. We will explore the challenges associated with the collection, storage, and use of personal data in the context of elections. We will discuss the potential risks of data breaches, the protection of voter information, and the role of legislation and international cooperation in ensuring data privacy and cybersecurity.

6. Digital Divide and Inclusivity

While technology has the potential to enhance democratic participation, it also highlights the existence of a digital divide that disproportionately affects marginalized communities. We will examine the challenges of ensuring equal access to digital tools and information, and the potential consequences of excluding certain segments of society from online political discourse. We will discuss strategies for bridging the digital divide and promoting inclusivity in the digital age.

7. Regulating Technology and Democratic Processes

This section will delve into the debate surrounding the regulation of technology and its impact on democratic processes. We will explore different approaches to regulating social media platforms, online political advertising, and data protection. We will discuss the balance between safeguarding democratic values, such as freedom of expression, and addressing the potential harms associated with unregulated technology.

Conclusion

Technology has reshaped the landscape of democratic governance, particularly in the realm of elections. Through this chapter, we have explored the transformative impact of technology on democracy, the opportunities it presents, and the challenges it poses. It is crucial for policymakers, technology companies, and civil society to work together to harness the positive potential of technology while addressing the risks and ensuring the integrity of democratic processes in the digital age.

Social Media and Political Campaigns

In the digital age, social media has emerged as a powerful tool that shapes political campaigns and influences democratic processes. This chapter explores the impact of social media on political campaigns, examining its role in candidate communication, voter engagement, mobilization, and the overall dynamics of modern political discourse. We will discuss the opportunities and challenges that social media presents, the effects on campaign strategies, and the implications for democratic governance.

1. The Rise of Social Media in Political Campaigns

We will begin by providing an overview of the rise of social media platforms in political campaigns. We will discuss the increasing prevalence of platforms such as Facebook, Twitter, Instagram, and YouTube as essential tools for political communication and engagement. We will explore how social media has transformed traditional campaign strategies, allowing for direct candidate-voter interaction and real-time dissemination of political messages.

2. Voter Engagement and Mobilization

Social media platforms have revolutionized the way political campaigns engage with voters and mobilize support. We will delve into the various ways social media enables campaigns to reach and connect with a broader audience, including targeted advertising, influencer endorsements, and grassroots mobilization efforts. We will discuss the benefits of increased voter engagement and the challenges of maintaining meaningful connections in an era of information overload.

3. The Influence of Social Media on Political Discourse

Social media platforms have reshaped the dynamics of political discourse by providing a space for diverse voices and opinions. We will examine how social media facilitates public conversations, promotes citizen journalism, and allows for rapid dissemination of news and information. However, we will also explore the challenges associated with echo chambers, filter bubbles, and the spread of misinformation in this decentralized digital space.

4. The Role of Social Media in Candidate Communication

Candidates now have direct access to their supporters and can use social media to shape their public image, share policy positions, and respond to current events. We will discuss the benefits and risks of this direct candidate-voter communication, examining how it affects transparency, authenticity, and accountability. We will also explore the challenges of managing online reputation and the potential for social media missteps to impact campaigns.

5. Data Analytics and Micro-targeting

Social media platforms collect vast amounts of user data, allowing campaigns to employ sophisticated data analytics and micro-targeting techniques. We will explore how campaigns use data-driven strategies to identify and reach specific voter segments, tailor messages, and maximize the effectiveness of their campaigns. We will discuss the ethical considerations surrounding data collection, privacy concerns, and the potential for manipulation.

6. Social Media and Political Activism

Social media has become a catalyst for political activism and social movements, empowering individuals to organize and voice their concerns. We will examine the role of social media in facilitating political protests, grassroots movements, and the mobilization of collective action. We will discuss the impact of social media in amplifying marginalized voices and driving social and political change.

7. Regulating Social Media in Political Campaigns

The influence of social media in political campaigns raises important questions about regulation and accountability. We will explore the challenges of regulating social media platforms, ensuring transparency in political advertising, and combating misinformation. We will discuss the role of government, technology companies, and civil society in developing effective regulations that preserve democratic values while addressing the risks associated with social media.

Conclusion

Social media has transformed political campaigns, presenting both opportunities and challenges for democratic governance. Through this chapter, we have explored the impact of social media on candidate communication, voter engagement, political discourse, and activism. It is essential for policymakers, technology companies, and citizens to navigate the complexities of social media in political campaigns to ensure its positive impact on democratic processes and outcomes.

Challenges of Cybersecurity and Election Interference

The digital age has brought significant advancements to democratic governance, but it has also introduced new challenges in the form of cybersecurity threats and election interference. This chapter delves into the complexities surrounding cybersecurity and the various ways in which malicious actors seek to undermine democratic processes. We will explore the vulnerabilities of digital systems, the techniques used for election interference, and the efforts taken to enhance cybersecurity and safeguard elections.

1. Understanding Cybersecurity in Democratic Systems

We will begin by providing a comprehensive understanding of cybersecurity in the context of democratic systems. This section will cover the fundamental concepts of cybersecurity, including the protection of information systems, networks, and data from unauthorized access, use, disclosure, disruption, modification, or destruction. We will explore the critical role of cybersecurity in maintaining the integrity, confidentiality, and availability of digital infrastructure for democratic governance.

2. Vulnerabilities in Digital Systems

Digital systems that underpin democratic processes are susceptible to a range of vulnerabilities. We will discuss common vulnerabilities, such as software vulnerabilities, weak network security, human error, and social engineering techniques. We will analyze the potential consequences of these vulnerabilities, including unauthorized access, data breaches, manipulation of information, and disruption of critical services.

3. Types of Election Interference

Election interference has become a significant concern in democratic societies. We will examine different types of election interference, including:

a. Cyber Attacks: This section will focus on the various forms of cyber attacks, such as distributed denial-of-service (DDoS) attacks, phishing, malware, and ransomware, which can compromise the integrity and availability of election systems.

b. Disinformation Campaigns: We will explore how disinformation campaigns, through the spread of false or misleading information, can manipulate public opinion, sow division, and undermine trust in democratic institutions.

c. Social Media Manipulation: This section will discuss the manipulation of social media platforms to disseminate misinformation, amplify divisive content, and target specific voter groups.

d. Foreign Influence Operations: We will examine the efforts of foreign entities to influence democratic processes through cyber operations, social media manipulation, and the funding of political campaigns.

4. Case Studies of Election Interference

Drawing on real-world examples, we will analyze notable case studies of election interference and cybersecurity breaches. These case studies may include instances of foreign interference in democratic elections, cyber attacks targeting electoral infrastructure, and disinformation campaigns aimed at shaping electoral outcomes. Through these case studies, we will highlight the strategies employed by malicious actors and the implications for democratic governance.

5. Enhancing Cybersecurity in Elections

To mitigate the risks of election interference, efforts are being made to enhance cybersecurity in electoral processes. We will explore the measures taken by governments, election commissions, and technology experts to protect the integrity of elections. This section will cover topics such as secure voter registration systems, robust election management systems, encryption and authentication mechanisms, and comprehensive incident response plans.

6. International Cooperation and Norms

Addressing cybersecurity challenges and election interference requires international cooperation and the establishment of norms and agreements. We will discuss the role of international organizations, such as the United Nations and the Organization for Security and Cooperation in Europe, in fostering cooperation among nations to combat cyber threats and protect democratic processes. We will also examine the challenges associated with establishing global norms in this complex and rapidly evolving landscape.

7. Balancing Security and Privacy

Efforts to enhance cybersecurity in elections must carefully balance security requirements with the protection of privacy rights. We will explore the tension between security measures, such as data collection and surveillance, and the need to uphold individual privacy and civil liberties. We will discuss the importance of transparency, accountability, and public trust in striking the right balance between security and privacy.

Conclusion

Cybersecurity threats and election interference pose significant challenges to democratic governance in the digital age. This chapter has explored the vulnerabilities in digital systems, the techniques used for election interference, and the efforts to enhance cybersecurity and safeguard elections. It is crucial for governments, electoral authorities, technology companies, and citizens to work collaboratively to strengthen cybersecurity measures, protect democratic processes, and preserve the integrity of elections in the face of evolving cyber threats.

Balancing Privacy and Security in the Digital Era

In the digital era, the balance between privacy and security has become a paramount concern for democratic societies. As technology advances and governments seek to protect national security interests, questions arise about the scope of surveillance, data collection, and the protection of individual privacy rights. This chapter delves into the intricate relationship between privacy and security, exploring the challenges, tensions, and potential solutions to strike the right balance in the digital age.

1. Understanding Privacy and Security in the Digital Era

To lay the foundation for the discussion, this section provides an overview of privacy and security in the context of democratic governance. It explores the definitions and concepts of privacy, including informational privacy, data protection, and individual rights. Similarly, it examines the concept of security, encompassing national security, cybersecurity, and public safety. By understanding the scope and significance of both privacy and security, we can better appreciate the challenges of balancing them in the digital era.

2. Evolving Technologies and Privacy Concerns

Technological advancements have revolutionized the way information is collected, stored, and analyzed. This section explores the impact of emerging technologies, such as artificial intelligence, biometrics, Internet of Things (IoT), and surveillance systems, on privacy. It highlights the privacy concerns associated with these technologies, including data breaches, mass surveillance, facial recognition, and algorithmic decision-making. Additionally, it examines the ethical and legal dimensions of privacy infringements in the digital age.

3. Government Surveillance and National Security

Governments worldwide grapple with the need to protect national security while respecting individual privacy rights. This section examines the various surveillance measures employed by governments, including mass surveillance programs, data retention laws, and intelligence gathering. It discusses the legal frameworks, such as anti-terrorism legislation, that govern government surveillance activities. The section also explores the challenges of oversight, accountability, and transparency in relation to government surveillance practices.

4. Data Collection and Privacy Risks

In the digital era, vast amounts of personal data are collected and processed by governments, corporations, and other entities. This section delves into the privacy risks associated with data collection practices, including data breaches, unauthorized access, profiling, and data monetization. It discusses the implications of data collection on individual privacy rights, autonomy, and the potential for discriminatory practices. Furthermore, it explores the role of consent, data protection regulations, and corporate responsibility in safeguarding privacy.

5. Encryption and Security Measures

Encryption plays a pivotal role in ensuring the security and privacy of digital communications and data. This section examines the importance of encryption in protecting sensitive information from unauthorized access and surveillance. It discusses the debates surrounding encryption backdoors, law enforcement access to encrypted data, and the balance between security needs and individual privacy rights. The section also explores other security measures, such as secure communication protocols and authentication mechanisms, in the digital era.

6. International Perspectives on Privacy and Security

Privacy and security concerns transcend national boundaries, requiring international cooperation and coordination. This section examines the approaches taken by different countries and regions to balance privacy and security in the digital era. It explores diverse regulatory frameworks, such as the European Union's General Data Protection Regulation (GDPR), as well as international agreements, like the Budapest Convention on Cybercrime. The section also discusses the challenges of harmonizing privacy and security standards in a globalized and interconnected world.

7. Public Trust, Transparency, and Accountability

Preserving public trust in democratic governance requires transparency and accountability in privacy and security practices. This section explores the importance of transparency, informing individuals about data collection and surveillance practices, and providing mechanisms for redress. It examines the role of independent oversight bodies, judicial review, and public consultation in ensuring accountability and checks on government surveillance activities. Additionally, it highlights the need for public education and awareness about privacy and security issues.

8. Future Directions and Recommendations

As technology continues to evolve rapidly, the challenges of balancing privacy and security in the digital era will persist. This section presents potential strategies and recommendations for navigating this complex landscape. It explores the role of technology companies, governments, civil society organizations, and individuals in finding the right balance. It discusses the need for comprehensive data protection regulations, strong encryption standards, and proactive privacy-enhancing technologies. The section also emphasizes the importance of an ongoing dialogue and collaboration between stakeholders to address emerging privacy and security challenges effectively.

Conclusion

Balancing privacy and security in the digital era is an ongoing and multifaceted challenge for democratic societies. This chapter has examined the complexities, tensions, and potential solutions in achieving this delicate balance. By respecting privacy rights while addressing legitimate security concerns, societies can uphold democratic values, protect individual liberties, and maintain public trust in the digital age. Through continued dialogue, policy development, and technological advancements, it is possible to navigate the evolving landscape of privacy and security and foster a democratic governance framework that safeguards both individual rights and collective security.

Conclusion

Recap of Key Insights on Western Democracies

In this comprehensive exploration of Western democracies, we have delved into various aspects of their political systems, challenges, and unique characteristics. Throughout the chapters, we have gained valuable insights into the significance of Western democracies in global politics, the historical evolution of democratic systems, challenges faced by democratic nations, and specific country profiles such as the United States, United Kingdom, Germany, and France. We have also examined the challenges to democracy in the digital age and the role of democratic institutions and civil society. As we conclude our journey, let us recap the key insights we have uncovered.

1. Significance of Western Democracies in Global Politics

Western democracies play a pivotal role in shaping the global political landscape. They serve as beacons of freedom, human rights, and democratic values, influencing other nations and promoting democratic governance worldwide. The stability, transparency, and accountability inherent in Western democracies make them essential actors in international relations, fostering cooperation, and upholding the rule of law on a global scale.

2. Historical Evolution of Democratic Systems

The historical evolution of democratic systems has been a complex and iterative process. From the ancient roots of democracy in Greece to the modern-day Western democracies, we have witnessed the emergence of different forms of government, the struggle for suffrage and equal representation, and the development of democratic institutions. Understanding this historical context provides us with a deeper appreciation of the principles and foundations that underpin Western democracies.

3. Challenges Faced by Democratic Nations

Despite their strengths, Western democracies are not immune to challenges. We have explored a range of obstacles that democratic nations encounter, including political polarization, populism, electoral reforms, and the rise of identity politics. By acknowledging and addressing these challenges, Western democracies can reinforce their democratic foundations and adapt to the changing needs of their societies.

4. Country Profiles: United States, United Kingdom, Germany, and France

Each country profile offers a unique perspective on democratic governance within the Western context. The United States, as a presidential system, exemplifies the separation of powers and the role of political parties. The United Kingdom showcases the parliamentary system and the influence of the monarchy. Germany's federal republic highlights coalition governments and proportional representation, while France's semi-presidential system emphasizes the power of the presidency. By examining these country profiles, we have gained valuable insights into the diversity of Western democratic systems.

5. Challenges to Democracy in the Digital Age

The digital age has presented both opportunities and challenges for democratic governance. We have explored the impact of technology on elections, the role of social media in political campaigns, cybersecurity threats, and the delicate balance between privacy and security. By recognizing and addressing these challenges, Western democracies can harness the potential of technology while safeguarding democratic values, ensuring transparency, and protecting citizens' rights.

6. Democratic Institutions and Civil Society

Democratic institutions, such as the judiciary and rule of law, play a crucial role in upholding democratic principles and maintaining checks and balances. We have examined the significance of an independent judiciary, the role of civil society organizations and interest groups, and the importance of a free and independent media. These institutions and civil society actors contribute to the vibrancy of Western democracies, ensuring accountability, and protecting citizens' rights.

7. The Future of Western Democracies

As we look ahead, it is essential to consider the future of Western democracies. Adapting to evolving challenges and embracing democratic innovations will be crucial in maintaining the vitality of democratic governance. This includes engaging citizens, promoting digital literacy, fostering inclusivity, and empowering marginalized communities. By strengthening democratic institutions, enhancing transparency, and nurturing active citizen participation, Western democracies can thrive in the face of future uncertainties.

In conclusion, our exploration of Western democracies has highlighted their significance, historical evolution, challenges, and unique characteristics. By understanding and addressing these insights, we can contribute to the preservation and enhancement of democratic governance in Western societies. As citizens, policymakers, and global citizens, it is our collective responsibility to uphold the values and principles that underpin Western democracies, ensuring that they remain resilient, inclusive, and responsive to the needs and aspirations of their citizens. By working together, we can navigate the complexities of the present and shape a brighter future for democratic governance in the Western world and beyond.

Future of Democracy and Potential Reforms

As we conclude our exploration of Western democracies and the challenges they face in the 21st century, it is essential to reflect on the future of democracy and the potential reforms that can shape its trajectory. Democracy, as a form of governance, is a dynamic and evolving concept that requires continuous adaptation to remain responsive and effective. In this final section, we will discuss key considerations and potential reforms that can help strengthen and advance democratic principles.

1. Strengthening Democratic Institutions

One crucial aspect of the future of democracy lies in the strengthening of democratic institutions. Institutions such as the judiciary, legislative bodies, and executive branches play a fundamental role in upholding democratic principles and maintaining checks and balances. Efforts should be made to ensure the independence and integrity of these institutions, promoting transparency, accountability, and the rule of law. Judicial reforms, whistleblower protection laws, and anti-corruption measures are some potential avenues for strengthening democratic institutions.

2. Enhancing Citizen Engagement and Participation

The future of democracy relies on active citizen engagement and participation. To ensure that the voices of all citizens are heard and their interests are represented, efforts should be made to promote inclusivity, diversity, and accessibility. This includes encouraging voter participation, expanding civic education programs, and fostering platforms for meaningful public deliberation. Citizen assemblies, participatory budgeting, and digital tools for direct democracy are potential reforms that can enhance citizen engagement and participation.

3. Embracing Technological Innovations

Technology has the potential to transform democratic processes and enhance citizen participation. Embracing technological innovations can increase transparency, streamline administrative procedures, and foster greater public engagement. E-voting systems, online consultations, and digital platforms for public deliberation are examples of technological reforms that can strengthen democracy. However, careful attention must be given to issues such as privacy, cybersecurity, and the digital divide to ensure that technology serves democratic values.

4. Addressing Political Polarization

Political polarization poses a significant challenge to democratic governance. It can hinder constructive dialogue, impede decision-making processes, and erode trust in democratic institutions. The future of democracy requires efforts to bridge divides, foster dialogue, and find common ground. Encouraging civil discourse, promoting media literacy, and supporting initiatives that promote empathy and understanding are potential strategies for addressing political polarization.

5. Advancing Electoral Reforms

Elections are the cornerstone of democratic systems, and ongoing electoral reforms are essential to ensure their integrity and fairness. Reforms can include updating electoral laws, enhancing campaign finance regulations, and exploring alternative voting systems. Proportional representation, ranked-choice voting, and campaign finance transparency are potential reforms that can strengthen the representativeness and legitimacy of electoral processes.

6. Strengthening International Cooperation

The future of democracy is not limited to national borders. In an interconnected world, collaboration among democratic nations is crucial. International cooperation can help address global challenges such as climate change, economic inequality, and migration. Strengthening alliances, promoting democratic values in international forums, and supporting democratic movements in authoritarian contexts are avenues for advancing democracy on a global scale.

7. Fostering Civic Education and Media Literacy

Civic education and media literacy are essential components of a thriving democracy. Educating citizens about democratic principles, the importance of informed decision-making, and critical thinking skills is crucial. Media literacy programs that promote fact-checking, media accountability, and responsible digital citizenship can empower citizens to navigate the complex media landscape and make informed judgments.

In conclusion, the future of democracy depends on our collective commitment to its principles and our willingness to adapt and reform. Strengthening democratic institutions, enhancing citizen engagement, embracing technological innovations, addressing political polarization, advancing electoral reforms, fostering international cooperation, and promoting civic education and media literacy are all crucial aspects of shaping the future of democracy. By embracing these potential reforms, we can build more inclusive, participatory, and resilient democratic systems that meet the challenges of the 21st century and uphold the values we hold dear. The journey to a stronger democracy requires ongoing dedication and active engagement from citizens, policymakers, civil society organizations, and international stakeholders. Together, we can shape a future where democracy thrives and continues to be a powerful force for progress, freedom, and justice.

Importance of Citizen Engagement and Democratic Participation

In the course of exploring Western democracies and the challenges they face, one recurring theme emerges: the crucial role of citizen engagement and democratic participation. Democracy thrives when citizens actively participate in the political process, voice their concerns, and contribute to decision-making. In this final section, we will delve into the significance of citizen engagement and democratic participation in ensuring the vitality and effectiveness of democratic systems.

1. The Foundation of Democracy: Citizen Sovereignty

At the heart of democracy lies the principle of citizen sovereignty. Democracy grants power to the people, and citizen engagement is the means by which individuals exercise their sovereign authority. By participating in elections, engaging in public discourse, and being informed about political issues, citizens contribute to shaping the policies and decisions that affect their lives. Citizen engagement is the bedrock upon which democracy stands.

2. Active Citizenship: Beyond Voting

While voting is a fundamental aspect of democratic participation, active citizenship extends beyond the act of casting a ballot. It encompasses a wide range of activities that allow citizens to influence the political process, hold elected officials accountable, and contribute to the development of public policies. Engaging in civil society organizations, participating in protests and demonstrations, and contacting elected representatives are examples of active citizenship that enrich democratic systems.

3. Fostering Inclusivity and Representation

Citizen engagement is vital for ensuring that democratic systems are inclusive and representative of diverse voices and interests. It allows marginalized communities, minority groups, and underrepresented populations to have their concerns heard and addressed. By actively engaging citizens from all walks of life, democracies can overcome systemic inequalities, promote social justice, and build a society that reflects the aspirations and needs of its entire population.

4. Enhancing Trust and Legitimacy

Citizen engagement is essential for building trust and legitimacy in democratic institutions. When citizens have opportunities to participate in decision-making processes, their trust in the democratic system and its outcomes is strengthened. Conversely, when citizens feel excluded or their voices go unheard, it can lead to disenchantment, apathy, and a decline in trust. Democratic systems must strive to create avenues for meaningful citizen engagement to foster trust and legitimacy.

5. Ensuring Accountability and Transparency

Citizen engagement serves as a check on power and promotes accountability in democratic systems. When citizens actively participate, they hold elected officials and government institutions accountable for their actions. Transparency and access to information are essential for citizen engagement to flourish. Robust mechanisms for reporting corruption, open government initiatives, and freedom of information laws are critical components of a transparent and accountable democracy.

6. Educating and Empowering Citizens

Citizen engagement is intimately linked to civic education and the empowerment of individuals to actively participate in democratic processes. Educating citizens about democratic values, political systems, and the importance of their role as active participants fosters informed decision-making and critical thinking. Civic education programs, media literacy initiatives, and inclusive educational curricula can equip citizens with the knowledge and skills necessary to engage meaningfully in democratic processes.

7. Democratic Participation in the Digital Age

The digital age has opened up new avenues for citizen engagement and democratic participation. Online platforms, social media, and digital tools offer opportunities for citizens to express their opinions, mobilize support for causes, and connect with like-minded individuals. However, the digital realm also presents challenges such as misinformation, echo chambers, and the digital divide. Safeguarding the integrity of digital spaces and ensuring equal access to technology are crucial for inclusive democratic participation.

In conclusion, citizen engagement and democratic participation are vital for the health and vibrancy of democratic systems. By actively engaging citizens, democracies can foster inclusivity, representation, trust, accountability, and transparency. Educating and empowering citizens, particularly in the digital age, strengthens democratic participation and ensures that the voices of all citizens are heard. As we navigate the challenges of the 21st century, it is through active citizen engagement that we can collectively shape the future of democracy and safeguard its core values for generations to come.

THE END

Key Terms and Definitions

To help you better understand the language and concepts related to aging and older adults, below you will find a list of key terms and their definitions.

key terms

1. Democracy: A system of government where power resides with the people, who exercise their authority through voting and participation in decision-making processes.

2. Western Democracies: Refers to democratic systems found in Western countries, such as the United States, the United Kingdom, Germany, and France. These democracies often share similar principles and institutions.

3. Electoral Systems: The rules and processes governing elections, including methods of voting, representation, and the allocation of seats in legislative bodies.

4. Party Politics: The activities, strategies, and competition among political parties in a democratic system, including campaigning, policy formation, and party platforms.

5. Challenges to Democracy: Refers to the obstacles, threats, and issues that democratic nations face in maintaining and strengthening their democratic systems,

such as populism, political polarization, and threats to freedom of the press.

6. Presidential System: A system of government in which the head of state and head of government is an elected president who holds executive powers separate from the legislature.

7. Parliamentary System: A system of government in which the executive branch is led by a prime minister or a similar official who is chosen from and accountable to the legislature.

8. Coalition Governments: Governments formed by two or more political parties that come together to gain a parliamentary majority and share power.

9. Proportional Representation: An electoral system in which the allocation of seats in a legislature is based on the proportion of votes each political party receives.

10. Role of the Monarchy: Refers to the position and functions of a monarch within a constitutional monarchy, where the monarch serves as a ceremonial head of state with limited or no political powers.

11. Devolution: The transfer of powers and responsibilities from a central government to regional or local governments within a country.

12. Brexit: The withdrawal of the United Kingdom from the European Union, following a referendum held in 2016.

13. Consensus Politics: A political approach that emphasizes reaching broad agreement and consensus among different political parties and interest groups.

14. Semi-Presidential System: A system of government where a president coexists with a prime minister and a cabinet, sharing executive powers.

15. Political Ideologies: Sets of beliefs and values that guide political behavior and shape policy preferences, such as liberalism, conservatism, socialism, and nationalism.

16. Electoral Laws: The regulations governing the conduct of elections, including rules on campaign financing, candidate eligibility, and electoral boundaries.

17. Populism: A political ideology or approach that appeals to the interests and concerns of ordinary people, often emphasizing the exclusion of elite or establishment groups.

18. Political Polarization: The division and intensification of political differences among individuals and groups, often leading to increased ideological and partisan conflict.

19. Freedom of Press: The right of journalists and media organizations to publish and disseminate information without censorship or undue interference from the government.

20. Civil Society Organizations: Non-governmental, non-profit organizations that operate independently of the state and pursue various social, cultural, or political objectives.

21. Digital Age: Refers to the current era characterized by the widespread use of digital technologies, including the internet, social media, and advanced communication tools.

22. Cybersecurity: Measures and practices aimed at protecting computer systems, networks, and data from unauthorized access, cyberattacks, and data breaches.

23. Citizen Engagement: The active involvement of citizens in public affairs, including political participation, civic activism, and community involvement.

24. Democratic Participation: The act of citizens contributing to decision-making processes, expressing their opinions, and participating in activities that shape the functioning of democratic systems.

Supporting Materials

Introduction

No specific references are provided in the introduction.

Chapter 1: United States

Dahl, R. A. (1971). Polyarchy: Participation and opposition. Yale University Press.

Diamond, L. (2005). Is the third wave of democratization over? An empirical assessment. Journal of Democracy, 16(2), 16-28.

Chapter 2: United Kingdom

Bogdanor, V. (2015). The British constitution in the twentieth century. Oxford University Press.

Dunleavy, P., & Diwakar, R. (2013). The UK coalition in power: A mid-term assessment. Parliamentary Affairs, 66(1), 160-178.

Chapter 3: Germany

Sturm, R. (2016). The Federal Republic of Germany: From division to reunification. Routledge.

Conradt, D. P., & Soe, C. M. (Eds.). (2017). The German polity. Rowman & Littlefield.

Chapter 4: France

Cole, A. (2016). French politics: A pragmatic analysis. Palgrave Macmillan.

Bell, D. S., & Criddle, B. (Eds.). (2016). Understanding French politics. Routledge.

Chapter 5: Challenges to Democracy

Levitsky, S., & Ziblatt, D. (2018). How democracies die. Crown.

Norris, P., & Inglehart, R. (2019). Cultural backlash: Trump, Brexit, and authoritarian populism. Cambridge University Press.

Chapter 6: Democratic Institutions and Civil Society

Ginsberg, B., Smith, K. E., & Tatalovich, R. (2017). Democracy in Western politics: Volume 1: National elections and the European Union. Routledge.

Keane, J. (2013). The life and death of democracy. Simon and Schuster.

Chapter 7: Democratic Governance in the Digital Age

Norris, P. (2017). Digital disruption? Party responses to online politics. Oxford Research Encyclopedia of Communication.

Chadwick, A. (2017). The hybrid media system: Politics and power. Oxford University Press.

Conclusion

No specific references are provided in the conclusion.

Milton Keynes UK
Ingram Content Group UK Ltd.
UKHW020651201023
430994UK00016B/564